A Work on the Proceedings of Pelagius

A Work on the Proceedings of Pelagius

St. Augustine

A Work on the Proceedings of Pelagius

© Lighthouse Publishing 2018

Written by: St. Augustine (Nov.13 354 – Aug.28 430)
Translated by Peter Holmes and Robert Ernest Wallis
Revised by: Professor Benjamin B. Warfield, D.D
Updated into Modern U.S English by A.M. Overett (b. 1960)

All rights reserved. Without limiting the rights under copyright reserved above, no part of this publication may be reproduced, stored in a retrieval system, or transmitted, in any form or by any means (electronic, mechanical, photocopying, recording or otherwise), without the prior written permission of the copyright owner of this book.

Published by
Lighthouse Christian Publishing
SAN 257-4330
5531 Dufferin Drive
Savage, Minnesota, 55378
United States of America

www.lighthousechristianpublishing.com

EXTRACT FROM AUGUSTIN'S "RETRACTATIONS," Book II. Chap. 45, ON THE FOLLOWING TREATISE, "DE GESTIS PELAGII." —

"About the same time, in the East (that is to say, in Palestinian Syria), Pelagius was summoned by certain catholic brethren before a tribunal of bishops, and was heard on his trial by fourteen prelates, in the absence of his accusers, who were unable to be present on the day of the synod. On his condemning the very dogmas which were read from the indictment against him, as assailing the grace of Christ, they pronounced him to be a catholic. But when the Acts of this synod found their way into our hands, I wrote a treatise on them, to prevent the idea gaining ground that, because he had been in a manner acquitted, his opinions also were approved by the bishops; or that the accused could by any chance have escaped condemnation at their hands, unless he had condemned the opinions charged against him. This treatise of mine begins with these words: 'After there came into my hands.'"

PREFACE TO THE BOOK ON THE PROCEEDINGS OF PELAGIUS.

In the year of Christ 415, Pelagius was accused of heresy in Palestine, and brought to trial on one or two occasions. At the first trial, which was held on or about the 30th of July, at a congress of his presbyters, by John, bishop of Jerusalem, no regular record was kept of the proceedings, as we are informed by Augustin in the following work (sec. 39 and 55). The hour and the day of this assembly we may learn from Orosius, a presbyter of Spain, who was present at the congress, and has in his Apology committed to writing some of its most memorable acts. We are informed by him that "after a great deal of earnest proceeding on both sides, the bishop John proposed the last resolution, that certain brethren should be sent with a letter to blessed Innocent, Pope of Rome, to the intent that he might decide on all the points which were to follow."

The second trial took place afterwards at Diospolis, a city in Palestine, before fourteen bishops, at which was kept an accurate record of the proceedings. The bishops are severally mentioned by Augustin in his work against Julianus, Book i. chs. v. and vii. (19, 32), in the following order: "Eulogius, John, Ammonianus, Porphyry, Eutonius, another Porphyry, Fidus, Zoninus, Zoboennus, Nymphidius, Chromatius, Jovinus, Eleutherius, and Clematius." There can be no doubt that Eulogius, bishop of Cæsarea, was also primate of the province of Palestine, because he is constantly mentioned by Augustin as occupying the first place before the other thirteen bishops, and even before John himself, bishop of Jerusalem.

We find from the epistle of Lucian, De revelatione corporis Stephani martyris, that this synod was held at the approach of Christmas. In this epistle he tells us of three visions which God had shown him in the year 415, —the first on December 3d, and the other two on the 10th and 17th of the same month; that he then reported the matter to John, bishop of Jerusalem, who sent him in quest of the martyr's sepulcher. He further informs us that he discovered the sepulcher, and at once returned to John, "who (says he) was attending a synod at Lydda, which is Diospolis." This must have happened about the 21st of the month, since Lucian goes on to say that John came, in the company of two more bishops, Eutonius of Sebaste and Eleutherius of Jericho, and that in their presence the relics of the martyr were removed on the 26th day of the same month of December.

A certain deacon, called Annianus, is supposed to have pleaded the cause of Pelagius at the synod; some learned men finding it easier to interpret of this deacon than of Pelagius what Jerome writes in a letter addressed to Alypius and Augustin (Epist. Augustinian. 202, 2): "For everything which he denies having ever uttered in that miserable synod of Diospolis he professes to hold in this work." Jerome bestowed the epithet of "miserable" on this synod of Diospolis, for no other reason (as we suppose) than because he discovered from its Acts how miserably the synod had been duped by Pelagius. Pope Innocent, after a sight of these Acts, expressly owned (see Epist. Augustinian. 183, 4) that "he could not bring himself to refuse either blame or praise of those bishops." Augustin, however, in the following treatise (see chs. 4

and 8), does not hesitate to call them "pious judges," and (in his first book against Julianus, i. ch. v. 19) "catholic judges," who, when Pelagius abjured the errors attributed to him, pronounced him a catholic, and acquitted him; indeed, he frequently cites these fourteen bishops as witnesses of the catholic faith in opposition to Julianus.

In his letters addressed to Pope Innocent in the year 416 (see Epist. Augustinian. 175, 4, and 177, 2), Augustin intimated that he knew nothing of the Proceedings of the synod except from hearsay; and in a letter to John, bishop of Jerusalem (Epist. 179, 4), he earnestly requested him to forward them to him. But the report was in his hands about midsummer in 417, when he wrote his Epistle to Paulinus (Epist. 186, 31); so that the date of the following treatise is thus traced to the commencement of the year 417, supposing it to have been published immediately after he had received the Proceedings.

The title given to this work by Augustin, in his book On Original Sin (15), stands De Gestis Palæstinis [On the Proceedings which took place in Palestine]; by this title Prosper likewise refers to the work (in his book Adv.Collatorem,43); but yet we ought to retain the inscription De Gestis Pelagii which is prefixed both to the ancient editions and to the particular Retractationin which Augustin reviewed this work. The treatise had this title given to it, no doubt, either because it had been already commonly accepted as a description of these proceedings of Pelagius and his vindication, which led to his boast that he had been acquitted; or else from the fact that an examination had become necessary of those proceedings, which the accused party had himself published in an abridged and garbled form. Hence Possidonius named the treatise by the title, Contra Gesta Pelagii [A Protest, or Vindication, against the Proceedings of Pelagius].

Out of this book Photius copied a very accurate account of the Synod of Diospolis and inserted it in his Bibliotheca (cod. 54). One may therefore conclude that this work of Augustin's is one of those which Possidonius, in his Life, ch. xi. or xxi., No. 59, mentions as having been "translated into the Greek tongue." The Aurelius to whom the work is dedicated is mentioned by Photius in the passage just cited, and by Prosper before him (in the 43d chapter of the above-quoted Adversus Collatorem), as "the bishop of Carthage." If the title page of old did not give them this information, they could both of them discover it from reading this book, especially ch. 23 [XI.].

A WORK ON THE PROCEEDINGS OF PELAGIUS

In One Book

ADDRESSED TO BISHOP AURELIUS [OF CARTHAGE], BY AURELIUS AUGUSTIN;

written about the commencement of the year, a.d.417.

The several heads of error which were alleged against Pelagius at the Synod in Palestine, with his answers to each charge, are minutely discussed. Augustin shows that, although Pelagius was acquitted by the synod, there still clave to him the suspicion of heresy; and that the acquittal of the accused by the synod was so contrived, that the heresy itself with which he was charged was unhesitatingly condemned.

Chapter 1. —Introduction.

After there came into my hands, holy father Aurelius, the ecclesiastical proceedings, by which fourteen bishops of the province of Palestine pronounced Pelagius a catholic, my hesitation, in which I was previously reluctant to make any lengthy or confident statement about the defense which he had made, came to an end. This defense, indeed, I had already read in a paper which he himself forwarded to me. Forasmuch, however, as I received no letter therewith from him, I was afraid that some discrepancy might be detected between my statement and the record of the ecclesiastical proceedings; and that, should Pelagius perhaps deny that he had sent me any paper (and it would have been difficult for me to prove that he had, when there was only one witness), I should rather seem guilty in the eyes of those who would readily credit his denial, either of an underhanded falsification, or else (to say the least) of a reckless credulity. Now, however, when I am to treat of matters which are shown to have actually transpired, and when, as it appears to me, all doubt is removed whether he really acted in the way described, your holiness, and everybody who reads these pages, will no doubt be able to judge, with greater readiness and certainty, both of his defense and of this my treatment of it.

Chapter 2 [I.]—The First Item in the Accusation, and Pelagius' Answer.

First of all, then, I offer to the Lord my God, who is also my defense and guide, unspeakable thanks, because I was not misled in my views respecting our holy brethren and fellow bishops who sat as judges in that case. His answers, indeed, they not without reason approved; because they had not to consider how he had in his writings stated the points which were objected against him, but what he had to say about them in his reply at the pending examination. A case of unsoundness in the faith is one thing, one of incautious statement is another thing. Now sundry objections were urged against Pelagius out of a written complaint, which our holy brethren and fellow-bishops in Gaul, Heros and Lazarus, presented, being themselves unable to be present, owing (as we afterwards learned from credible information) to the severe indisposition of one of them. The first of these was, that he writes, in a certain book of his, this: "No man can be without sin unless he has acquired a knowledge of the law." After this had been read out, the synod inquired: "Did you, Pelagius, express yourself thus?" Then in answer he said: "I certainly used the words, but not in the sense in which they understand them. I did not say that a man is unable to sin who has acquired a knowledge of the law; but that he is by the knowledge of the law assisted towards not sinning, even as it is written, 'He hath given them a law for help'" Upon hearing this, the synod declared: "The words which have been spoken by Pelagius are not different from the Church." Assuredly they are not different, as he expressed them in his answer; the statement, however, which was produced from his book has a different meaning. But this the bishops, who were Greek-speaking men, and who heard the words through an interpreter, were not concerned with discussing. All they had to consider at the moment was, what the man who was under examination said was his meaning, —not in what words his opinion was alleged to have been expressed in his book.

Chapter 3. —Discussion of Pelagius' First Answer.

Now to say that "a man is by the knowledge of the law assisted towards not sinning," is a different assertion from saying that "a man cannot be without sin unless he has acquired a knowledge of the law." We see, for example, that corn-floors may be threshed without threshing-sledges,—however much these may assist the operation if we have them; and that boys can find their way to school without the pedagogue,—however valuable for this may be the office of pedagogues; and that many persons recover from sickness without physicians,—although the doctor's skill is clearly of greatest use; and that men sometimes live on other aliments besides bread,—however valuable the use of bread must needs be allowed to be; and many other illustrations may occur to the thoughtful reader, without our prompting. From which examples we are undoubtedly reminded that there are two sorts of aids. Some are indispensable, and without their help the desired result could not be attained. Without a ship, for instance, no man could take a voyage; no man could speak without a voice; without legs no man could walk; without light nobody could see; and so on in numberless instances. Amongst them this also may be reckoned, that without God's grace no man can live rightly. But then, again, there are other helps, which render us assistance in such a way that we might in some other way effect the object to which they are ordinarily auxiliary in their absence. Such are those which I have already mentioned, —the threshing-sledges for threshing corn, the pedagogue for conducting the child, medical art applied to the recovery of health, and other like instances. We have therefore to inquire to which of these two classes belongs the knowledge of the law, —in other words, to consider in what way it helps us towards the avoidance of sin. If it be in the sense of indispensable aid without which the end cannot be attained; not only was Pelagius' answer before the judges true, but what he wrote in his book was true also. If, however, it be of such a character that it helps indeed if it is present, but even if it be absent, then the result is still possible to be attained by some other means,—his answer to the judges was still true, and not unreasonably did it find favor with the bishops that "man is assisted not to sin by the knowledge of the law;"

but what he wrote in his book is not true, that "there is no man without sin except him who has acquired a knowledge of the law,"—a statement which the judges left undiscussed, as they were ignorant of the Latin language, and were content with the confession of the man who was pleading his cause before them, especially as no one was present on the other side who could oblige the interpreter to expose his meaning by an explanation of the words of his book, and to show why it was that the brethren were not groundlessly disturbed. For but very few persons are thoroughly acquainted with the law. The mass of the members of Christ, who are scattered abroad everywhere, being ignorant of the very profound and complicated contents of the law, are commended by the piety of simple faith and unfailing hope in God, and sincere love. Endowed with such gifts, they trust that by the grace of God they may be purged from their sins through our Lord Jesus Christ.

Chapter 4 [II.]—The Same Continued.

If Pelagius, as he possibly might, were to say in reply to this, that that very thing was what he meant by "the knowledge of the law, without which a man is unable to be free from sins," which is communicated by the teaching of faith to converts and to babes in Christ, and in which candidates for baptism are catechetically instructed with a view to their knowing the creed, certainly this is not what is usually meant when any one is said to have a knowledge of the law. This phrase is only applied to such persons as are skilled in the law. But if he persists in describing the knowledge of the law by the words in question, which, however few in number, are great in weight, and are used to designate all who are faithfully baptized according to the prescribed rule of the Churches; and if he maintains that it was of this that he said, "No one is without sin, but the man who has acquired the knowledge of the law,"—a knowledge which must needs be conveyed to believers before they attain to the actual remission of sins,—even in such case there would crowd around him a countless multitude, not indeed of angry disputants, but of crying baptized infants, who would exclaim,—not, to be sure, in words, but in the very truthfulness of innocence,—"What is it, O what is it that you have written: 'He only can be without sin who has acquired a knowledge of the law?' See here are we, a large flock of lambs, without sin, and yet we have no knowledge of the law." Now surely they with their silent tongue would compel him to silence, or, perhaps, even to confess that he was corrected of his great perverseness; or else (if you will), that he had already for some time entertained the opinion which he acknowledged before his ecclesiastical examiners, but that he had failed before to express his opinion in words of sufficient care, —that his faith, therefore, should be approved, but this book revised and amended. For, as the Scripture says: "There is that slipped in his speech, but not in his heart." Now if he would only admit this, or were already saying it, who would not most readily forgive those words which he had committed to writing with too great heedlessness and neglect, especially on his declining to defend the opinion which the said words contain, and affirming that to be his proper view which the truth approves? This we must suppose would have been in the minds of the pious judges themselves, if they could only have duly understood the contents of his Latin book, thoroughly interpreted to them, as they understood his reply to the synod, which was spoken in Greek, and therefore quite intelligible to them, and adjudged it as not alien from the Church. Let us go on to consider the other cases.

Chapter 5 [III.]—The Second Item in the Accusation; And Pelagius' Answer.

The synod of bishops then proceeded to say: "Let another section be read." Accordingly, there was read the passage in the same book wherein Pelagius had laid down the position that "all men are ruled by their own will." On this being read, Pelagius said in answer: "This I stated in the interest of free will. God is its helper whenever it chooses good; man, however, when sinning is himself in fault, as under the direction of a free will." Upon hearing this, the bishops exclaimed: "Nor again is this opposed to the doctrine of the Church." For who indeed could condemn or deny the freedom of the will, when God's help is associated with it? His opinion, therefore, as thus explained in his answer, was, with good reason, deemed satisfactory by the bishops. And yet, after all, the statement made in his book, "All men are ruled by their own will," ought without doubt to have deeply disturbed the brethren, who had discovered what these men are accustomed to dispute against the grace of God. For it is said, "All men are ruled by their own will," as if God rules no man, and the Scripture says in vain, "Save Thy people, and bless Thine inheritance; rule them, and lift them up forever." They would not, of course, stay, if they are ruled only by their own will without God, even as sheep which have no shepherd: which, God forbid for us. For, unquestionably to be led is something more compulsory than to be ruled. He who is ruled at the same time does something himself, —indeed, when ruled by God, it is with the express view that he should also act rightly; whereas the man who is led can hardly be understood to do anything himself at all. And yet the Savior's helpful grace is so much better than our own wills and desires, that the apostle does not hesitate to say: "As many as are led by the Spirit of God, they are the sons of God." And our free will can do nothing better for us than to submit itself to be led by Him who can do nothing amiss; and after doing this, not to doubt that it was helped to do it by Him of whom it is said in the psalm, "He is my God, His mercy shall go before me."

Chapter 6. —Pelagius' Answer Examined.

Indeed, in this very book which contains these statements, after laying down the position, "All men are governed by their own will, and everyone is submitted to his own desire," Pelagius goes on to adduce the testimony of Scripture, from which it is evident enough that no man ought to trust to himself for direction. For on this very subject the Wisdom of Solomon declares: "I myself also am a mortal man like unto all; and the offspring of him that was first made of the earth,"—with other similar words to the conclusion of the paragraph, where we read: "For all men have one entrance into life, and the like going out therefrom: wherefore I prayed and understanding was given to me; I called, and the Spirit of Wisdom came into me." Now is it not clearer than light itself, how that this man, on duly considering the wretchedness of human frailty, did not dare to commit himself to his own direction, but prayed, and understanding was given to him, concerning which the apostle says: "But we have the understanding of the Lord;" and called, and the Spirit of Wisdom entered into him? Now it is by this Spirit, and not by the strength of their own will, that they who are God's children are governed and led.

Chapter 7. —The Same Continued.

As for the passage from the psalm, "He loved cursing, and it shall come upon him; and he willed not blessing, so it shall be far removed from him," which he quoted in the same book of Chapters, as if to prove that "all men are ruled by their own will," who can be ignorant that this is a fault not of nature as God created it, but of human will which departed from God? The fact indeed is, that even if he had not loved cursing, and had willed blessing, he would in this very case, too, deny that his will had received any assistance from God; in his ingratitude and impiety, moreover, he would submit himself to be ruled by himself, until he found out by his penalties that, sunk as he was into ruin, without God to govern him he was utterly unable to direct his own self. In like manner, from the passage which he quoted in the same book under the same head, "He hath set fire and water before thee; stretch forth thy hand unto whether thou wilt; before man are good and evil, life and death, and whichever he liked shall be given to him," it is manifest that, if he applies his hand to fire, and if evil and death please him, his human will effects all this; but if, on the contrary, he loves goodness and life, not alone does his will accomplish the happy choice, but it is assisted by divine grace. The eye indeed is sufficient for itself, for not seeing, that is, for darkness; but for seeing, it is in its own light not sufficient for itself unless the assistance of a clear external light is rendered to it. God forbid, however, that they who are "the called according to His purpose, whom He also foreknew, and predestinated to be conformed to the likeness of His Son," should be given up to their own desire to perish. This is suffered only by "the vessels of wrath," who are perfected for perdition; in whose very destruction, indeed, God "makes known the riches of His glory on the vessels of His mercy." Now it is on this account that, after saying, "He is my God, His mercy shall go before me," he immediately adds, "My God will show me vengeance upon my enemies." That therefore happens to them which is mentioned in Scripture, "God gave them up to the lusts of their own heart." This, however, does not happen to the predestinated, who are ruled by the Spirit of God, for not in vain is their cry: "Deliver me not, O Lord, to the sinner, according to my desire." With regard, indeed, to the evil lusts which assail them, their prayer has ever assumed some such shape as this: "Take away from me the concupiscence of the belly; and let not the desire of lust take hold of me." Upon those whom He governs as His subjects does God bestow this gift; but not upon those who think themselves capable of governing themselves, and who, in the stiff-necked confidence of their own will, disdain to have Him as their ruler.

Chapter 8. —The Same Continued.

This being the case, how must God's children, who have learned the truth of all this and rejoice at being ruled and led by the Spirit of God, have been affected when they heard or read that Pelagius had declared in writing that "all men are governed by their own will, and that everyone is submitted to his own desire?" And yet, when questioned by the bishops, he fully perceived what an evil impression these words of his might produce, and told them in answer that "he had made such an assertion in the interest of free will,"—adding at once, "God is its helper whenever it chooses good; whilst man is himself in fault when he sins, as being under the influence of a free will." Although the pious judges approved of this sentiment also, they were unwilling to consider or examine how incautiously he had written, or indeed in what sense he had employed the words found in his book. They thought it was enough that he had made such a confession concerning free will, as to admit that God helped the man who chose the good, whereas the man who sinned was himself to blame, his own will sufficing for him in this direction. According to this, God rules those whom He assists in their choice of the good. So far, then, as they rule anything themselves, they rule it rightly, since they themselves are ruled by Him who is right and good.

Chapter 9. —The Third Item in the Accusation; And Pelagius' Answer.

Another statement was read which Pelagius had placed in his book, to this effect: "In the day of judgment no forbearance will be shown to the ungodly and the sinners, but they will be consumed in eternal fires." This induced the brethren to regard the statement as open to the objection, that it seemed so worded as to imply that all sinners whatever were to be punished with an eternal punishment, without excepting even those who hold

Christ as their foundation, although "they build thereupon wood, hay, stubble," concerning whom the apostle writes: "If any man's work shall be burned, he shall suffer loss; but he shall himself be saved, yet so as by fire." When, however, Pelagius responded that "he had made his assertion in accordance with the Gospel, in which it is written concerning sinners, 'These shall go away into eternal punishment, but the righteous into life eternal,'" it was impossible for Christian judges to be dissatisfied with a sentence which is written in the Gospel, and was spoken by the Lord; especially as they knew not what there was in the words taken from Pelagius' book which could so disturb the brethren, who were accustomed to hear his discussions and those of his followers. Since also they were absent who presented the indictment against Pelagius to the holy bishop Eulogius, there was no one to urge him that he ought to distinguish, by some exception, between those sinners who are to be saved by fire, and those who are to be punished with everlasting perdition. If, indeed, the judges had come to understand by these means the reason why the objection had been made to his statement, had he then refused to allow the distinction, he would have been justly open to blame.

Chapter 10. —Pelagius' Answer Examined. On Origen's Error Concerning the Non- Eternity of the Punishment of the Devil and the Damned.

But what Pelagius added, "Who believes differently is an Origenist," was approved by the judges, because in very deed the Church most justly abominates the opinion of Origen, that even they whom the Lord says are to be punished with everlasting punishment, and the devil himself and his angels, after a time, however protracted, will be purged, and released from their penalties, and shall then cleave to the saints who reign with God in the association of blessedness. This additional sentence, therefore, the synod pronounced to be "not opposed to the Church,"—not in accordance with Pelagius, but rather in accordance with the Gospel, that such ungodly and sinful men shall be consumed by eternal fires as the Gospel determines to be worthy of such a punishment; and that he is a sharer in Origen's abominable opinion, who affirms that their punishment can possibly ever come to an end, when the Lord has said it is to be eternal. Concerning those sinners, however, of whom the apostle declares that "they shall be saved, yet so as by fire, after their work has been burnt up," inasmuch as no objectionable opinion about them was manifestly charged against Pelagius, the synod determined nothing. Wherefore he who says that the ungodly and sinner, whom the truth consigns to eternal punishment, can ever be liberated therefrom, is not unfitly designated by Pelagius as an "Origenist." But, on the other hand, he who supposes that no sinner whatever deserves mercy in the judgment of God, may be designated by whatever name Pelagius is disposed to give to him, only it must at the same time be quite understood that this error is not received as truth by the Church. "For he shall have judgment without mercy that hath showed no mercy."

Chapter 11. —The Same Continued.

But how this judgment is to be accomplished, it is not easy to understand from Holy Scripture; for there are many modes therein of describing that which is to come to pass only in one mode. In one place the Lord declares that He will "shut the door" against those whom He does not admit into His kingdom; and that, on their clamorously demanding admission, "Open unto us, . . . we have eaten and drunk in Thy presence," and so forth, as the Scripture describes, "He will say unto them in answer, I know you not, . . . all ye workers of iniquity." In another passage He reminds us that He will command "all which would not that He should reign over them to be brought to Him, and be slain in His presence." In another place, again, He tells us that He will come with His angels in His majesty; and before Him shall be gathered all nations, and He shall separate them one from another; some He will set on His right hand, and after enumerating their good works, will award to them eternal life; and others on His left hand, whose barrenness in all good works He will expose, will He condemn to everlasting fire. In two other passages He deals with that wicked and slothful servant, who neglected to trade with His money, and with the man who was found at the feast without the wedding garment, —and He orders them to be bound hand and foot, and to be cast into outer darkness. And in yet another scripture, after admitting the five virgins who were wise, He shuts the door against the other five foolish ones. Now these descriptions, —and there are others which at the instant do not occur to me, —are all intended to represent to us the future judgment, which of course will be held not over one, or over five, but over multitudes. For if it were a solitary case only of the man who was cast into outer darkness for not having on the wedding garment, He would not have gone on at once to give it a plural turn, by saying: "For many are called, but few are chosen;"

whereas it is plain that, after the one was cast out and condemned, many still remained behind in the house. However, it would occupy us too long to discuss all these questions to the full. This brief remark, however, I may make, without prejudice (as they say in pecuniary affairs) to some better discussion, that by the many descriptions which are scattered throughout the Holy Scriptures there is signified to us but one mode of final judgment, which is inscrutable to us, —with only the variety of deservings preserved in the rewards and punishments. Touching the particular point, indeed, which we have before us at present, it is sufficient to remark that, if Pelagius had actually said that all sinners whatever without exception would be punished in an eternity of punishment by everlasting fire, then whosoever had approved of this judgment would, to begin with, have brought the sentence down on his own head. "For who will boast that he is pure from sins?" Forasmuch, however, as he did not say all, nor certain, but made an indefinite statement only, —and afterwards, in explanation, declared that his meaning was according to the words of the Gospel, —his opinion was affirmed by the judgment of the bishops to be true; but it does not even now appear what Pelagius really thinks on the subject, and in consequence there is no indecency in inquiring further into the decision of the episcopal judges.

Chapter 12 [IV.]—The Fourth Item in the Accusation; And Pelagius' Answer.

It was further objected against Pelagius, as if he had written in his book, that "evil does not enter our thoughts." In reply, however, to this charge, he said: "We made no such statement. What we did say was, that the

Christian ought to be careful not to have evil thoughts." Of this, as it became them, the bishops approved. For who can doubt that evil ought not to be thought of? And, indeed, if what he said in his book about "evil not being thought" runs in this form, "neither is evil to be thought of," the ordinary meaning of such words is "that evil ought not even to be thought of." Now if any person denies this, what else does he in fact say, than that evil ought to be thought of? And if this were true, it could not be said in praise of love that "it thinketh no evil!" But after all, the phrase about "not entering into the thoughts" of righteous and holy men is not quite a commendable one, for this reason, that what enters the mind is commonly called a thought, even when assent to it does not follow. The thought, however, which contracts blame, and is justly forbidden, is never unaccompanied with assent. Possibly those men had an incorrect copy of Pelagius' writings, who thought it proper to object to him that he had used the words: "Evil does not enter into our thoughts;" that is, that whatever is evil never enters into the thoughts of righteous and holy men. Which is, of course, a very absurd statement. For whenever we censure evil things, we cannot enunciate them in words, unless they have been thought. But, as we said before, that is termed a culpable thought of evil which carries with it assent.

Chapter 13 [V.]—The Fifth Item of the Accusation; And Pelagius' Answer.

After the judges had accorded their approbation to this answer of Pelagius, another passage which he had written in his book was read aloud: "The kingdom of heaven was promised even in the Old Testament." Upon this, Pelagius remarked in vindication: "This can be proved by the Scriptures: but heretics, in order to disparage the Old Testament, deny this. I, however, simply followed the authority of the Scriptures when I said this; for in the prophet Daniel it is written: 'The saints shall receive the kingdom of the Most. High.'" After they had heard this answer, the synod said: "Neither is this opposed to the Church's faith."

Chapter 14. —Examination of This Point. The Phrase "Old Testament" Used in Two Senses. The Heir of the Old Testament. In the Old Testament There Were Heirs of the New Testament.

Was it therefore without reason that our brethren were moved by his words to include this charge among the others against him? Certainly not. The fact is, that the phrase Old Testament is constantly employed in two different ways, —in one, following the authority of the Holy Scriptures; in the other, following the most common custom of speech. For the Apostle Paul says, in his Epistle to the Galatians: "Tell me, ye that desire to be under the law, do ye not hear the law? For it is written that Abraham had two sons, the one by a bondmaid, the other by a free woman...Which things are an allegory: for these are the two testaments; the one which gendered to bondage, which is Agar. For this is Mount Sinai in Arabia, and is conjoined with the Jerusalem which now is, and is in bondage with her children; whereas the Jerusalem which is above is free, and is the mother of us all." Now, inasmuch as the Old Testament belongs to bondage, whence it is written, "Cast out the bond-woman and her son, for the son of the bond-woman shall not be heir with my son Isaac," but the kingdom of heaven to liberty; what has the kingdom of heaven to do with the Old Testament? Since, however, as I have already remarked, we are accustomed, in our ordinary use of words, to designate all those Scriptures of the law and the prophets which were given previous to the Lord's incarnation, and are embraced together by canonical authority, under the name and title of the Old Testament, what man who is ever so moderately informed in ecclesiastical lore can be ignorant that the kingdom of heaven could be quite as well promised in those early Scriptures as even the New Testament itself, to which the kingdom of heaven belongs? At all events, in those ancient Scriptures it is most distinctly written: "Behold, the days come, saith the Lord, that I will consummate a new testament with the house of Israel and with the house of Jacob; not according to the testament that I made with their fathers, in the day that I took them by the hand, to lead them out of the land of Egypt." This was done on Mount Sinai. But then there had not yet risen the prophet Daniel to say: "The saints shall receive the kingdom of the Most High." For by these words he foretold the merit not of the Old, but of the New Testament. In the same manner did the same prophets foretell that Christ Himself would come, in whose blood the New Testament was consecrated. Of this Testament also the apostles became the ministers, as the most blessed Paul declares: "He hath made us able ministers of the New Testament; not in its letter, but in spirit: for the letter kills, but the spirit gives life." In that testament, however, which is properly called the Old, and was given on Mount Sinai, only earthly happiness is expressly promised. Accordingly that land, into which the nation, after being led through the wilderness, was conducted, is called the land of promise, wherein peace and royal power, and the gaining of victories over enemies, and an abundance of children and of fruits of the ground, and gifts of a similar kind are the promises of the Old Testament. And these, indeed, are figures of the spiritual blessings which appertain to the New Testament; but yet the man who lives under God's law with those earthly blessings for his sanction, is precisely the heir of the Old Testament, for just such rewards are promised and given to him, according to the terms of the Old Testament, as are the objects of his desire according to the condition of the old man. But whatever blessings are there figuratively set forth as appertaining to the New Testament require the new man to give them effect. And no doubt the great apostle understood perfectly well what he was saying, when he described the two testaments as capable of the allegorical distinction of the bond-woman and the free, —attributing the children of the flesh to the Old, and to the New the children of the promise: "They," says he, "which are the children of the flesh, are not the children of God; but the children of the promise are counted for the seed." The children of the flesh, then, belong to the earthly Jerusalem, which is in bondage with her children; whereas the children of the promise belong to the Jerusalem above, the free, the mother of us all, eternal in the heavens. Whence we can easily see who they are that appertain to the earthly, and who to the heavenly kingdom. But then the happy persons, who even in that early age were by the grace of God taught to understand the distinction now set forth, were thereby made the children of promise, and were accounted in the secret purpose of God as heirs of the New Testament; although they continued with perfect fitness to administer the Old Testament to the ancient people of God, because it was divinely appropriated to that people in God's distribution of the times and seasons.

Chapter 15. —The Same Continued.

How then should there not be a feeling of just disquietude entertained by the children of promise, children of the free Jerusalem, which is eternal in the heavens, when they see that by the words of Pelagius the distinction which has been drawn by Apostolic and catholic authority is abolished, and Agar is supposed to be by some means on a par with Sarah? He therefore does injury to the scripture of the Old Testament with heretical impiety, who with an impious and sacrilegious face denies that it was inspired by the good, supreme, and very God, —as Marcion does, as Manichæus does, and other pests of similar opinions. On this account (that I may put into as brief a space as I can what my own views are on the subject), as much injury is done to the New Testament, when it is put on the same level with the Old Testament, as is inflicted on the Old itself when men deny it to be the work of the supreme God of goodness. Now, when Pelagius in his answer gave as his reason for saying that even in the Old Testament there was a promise of the kingdom of heaven, the testimony of the prophet Daniel, who most plainly foretold that the saints should receive the kingdom of the Most High, it was fairly decided that the statement of Pelagius was not opposed to the catholic faith, although not according to the distinction which shows that the earthly promises of Mount Sinai are the proper characteristics of the Old Testament; nor indeed was the decision an improper one, considering that mode of speech which designates all the canonical Scriptures which were given to men before the Lord's coming in the flesh by the title of the "Old Testament." The kingdom of the Most High is of course none other than the kingdom of God; otherwise, anybody might boldly contend that the kingdom of God is one thing, and the kingdom of heaven another.

Chapter 16 [VI.]—The Sixth Item of the Accusation, and Pelagius' Reply.

The next objection was to the effect that Pelagius in that same book of his wrote thus: "A man is able, if he likes, to be without sin;" and that writing to a certain widow he said, flatteringly: "In thee piety may find a dwelling-place, such as she finds nowhere else; in thee righteousness, though a stranger, can find a home; truth, which no one any longer recognizes, can discover an abode and a friend in thee; and the law of God, which almost everybody despises, may be honored by thee alone." And in another sentence he writes to her: "O how happy and blessed art thou, when that righteousness which we must believe to flourish only in heaven has found a shelter on earth only in thy heart!" In another work addressed to her, after reciting the prayer of our Lord and Savior Jesus Christ, and teaching her in what manner saints ought to pray, he says: "He worthily raises his hands to God, and with a good conscience does he pour out his prayer, who is able to say, 'Thou, O Lord, knows how holy, and harmless, and pure from all injury and iniquity and violence, are the hands which I stretch out to Thee; how righteous, and pure, and free from all deceit, are the lips with which I offer to Thee my supplication, that Thou wouldst have mercy upon me.'" To all this Pelagius said in answer: "We asserted that a man could be without sin, and could keep God's commandments if he wished; for this capacity has been given to him by God. But we never said that any man could be found who at no time whatever, from infancy to old age, had committed sin: but that if any person were converted from his sins, he could by his own labor and God's grace be without sin; and yet not even thus would he be incapable of change ever afterwards. As for the other statements which they have made against us, they are not to be found in our books, nor have we at any time said such things." Upon hearing this vindication, the synod put this question to him: "You have denied having ever written such words; are you therefore ready to anathematize those who do hold these opinions?" Pelagius answered: "I anathematize them as fools, not as heretics, for there is no dogma." The bishops then pronounced their judgment in these words: "Since now Pelagius has with his own mouth anathematized this vague statement as foolish verbiage, justly declaring in his reply, 'That a man is able with God's assistance and grace to be without sin,' let him now proceed to answer the other heads of accusation against him."

Chapter 17. —Examination of the Sixth Charge and Answers.

Well, now, had the judges either the power or the right to condemn these unrecognized and vague words, when no person on the other side was present to assert that Pelagius had written the very culpable sentences which were alleged to have been addressed by him to the widow? In such a matter, it surely could not be enough to produce a manuscript, and to read out of it words as his, if there were not also witnesses forthcoming in case he denied, on the words being read out, that they ever dropped from his pen. But even here the judges did all that lay in their power to do, when they asked Pelagius whether he would anathematize the persons who held such sentiments as he declared he had never himself propounded either in speech or in writing. And when he answered that he did anathematize them as fools, what right had the judges to push the inquiry any further on the matter, in the absence of Pelagius' opponents?

Chapter 18. —The Same Continued.

But perhaps the point requires some consideration, whether he was right in saying that "such as held the opinions in question deserved anathema, not as heretics, but as fools, since it was no dogma." The question, when fairly confronted, is no doubt far from being an unimportant one, —how far a man deserves to be described as a heretic; on this occasion, however, the judges acted rightly in abstaining from it altogether. If anyone, for example, were to allege that eaglets are suspended in the talons of the parent bird, and so exposed to the rays of the sun, and such as wink are flung to the ground as spurious, the light being in some mysterious way the gauge of their genuine nature, he is not to be accounted a heretic, if the story happens to be untrue. And, since it occurs in the writings of the learned and is very commonly received as fact, ought it to be considered a foolish thing to mention it, even though it be not true? much less ought our credit, which gains for us the name of being trustworthy, to be affected, on the one hand injuriously if the story be believed by us, or beneficially if disbelieved. If, to go a step further in illustration, anyone were from this opinion to contend that there existed in birds reasonable souls, from the notion that human souls at intervals passed into them, then indeed we should have to reject from our mind and ears alike an idea like this as the rankest heresy; and even if the story about the eagles were true (as there are many curious facts about bees before our eyes, that are true), we should still have to consider, and demonstrate, the great difference that exists between the condition of creatures like these, which are quite irrational, however surprising in their powers of sensation, and the nature which is common (not to men and beasts, but) to men and angels. There are, to be sure, a great many foolish things said by foolish and ignorant persons, which yet fail to prove them heretics. One might instance the silly talk so commonly heard about the pursuits of other people, from persons who have never learned these pursuits, —equally hasty and untenable whether in the shape of excessive and indiscriminate praise of those they love, or of blame in the case of those they happen to dislike. The same remark might be made concerning the usual current of human conversation: whenever it does touch on a subject which requires dogmatic accuracy of statement, but is thrown out at random or suggested by the passing moment, it is too often pervaded by foolish levity, whether uttered by the mouth or expressed in writing. Many persons, indeed, when gently reminded of their reckless gossip, have afterwards much regretted their conduct; they scarcely recollected what they had never uttered with a fixed purpose, but had poured forth in a sheer volley of casual and unconsidered words. It is, unhappily, almost impossible to be quite clear of such faults. Who is he "that slipped not in his tongue," and "offended not in word?" It, however, makes all the difference in the world, to what extent, and from what motive, and whether in fact at all, a man when warned of his fault corrects it, or obstinately clings to it so as to make a dogma and settled opinion of that which he had not at first uttered on purpose, but only in levity. Although, then, it turns out eventually that every heretic is a fool, it does not follow that every fool must immediately be named a heretic. The judges were quite right in saying that Pelagius had anathematized the vague folly under consideration by its fitting designation for even if it were heresy, there could be no doubt of its being foolish prattle. Whatever, therefore, it was, they designated the offence under a general name. But whether the quoted words had been used with any definitely dogmatic purpose, or only in a vague and indeterminate sense, and with an unmeaningness which should be capable of an easy correction, they did not deem it necessary to discuss on the present occasion, since the man who was on his trial before them denied that the words were his at all, in whatever sense they had been employed.

Chapter 19. —The Same Continued.

Now it so happened that, while we were reading this defense of Pelagius in the small paper which we received at first, there were present certain holy brethren, who said that they had in their possession some hortatory or consolatory works which Pelagius had addressed to a widow lady whose name did not appear, and they advised us to examine whether the words which he had abjured for his own occurred anywhere in these books. They were not themselves aware whether they did or not. The said books were accordingly read through, and the words in question were actually discovered in them. Moreover, they who had produced the copy of the book, affirmed that for now almost four years they had had these books as Pelagius', nor had they once heard a doubt expressed about his authorship. Considering, then, from the integrity of these servants of God, which was very well known to us, how impossible it was for them to use deceit in the matter, the conclusion seemed inevitable, that Pelagius must be supposed by us to have rather been the deceiver at his trial before the bishops; unless we should think it possible that something may have been published, even for so many years, in his name, although not actually composed by him; for our informants did not tell us that they had received the books from Pelagius himself, nor had they ever heard him admit his own authorship. Now, in my own case, certain of our brethren have told me that sundry writings have found their way into Spain under my name. Such persons, indeed, as had read my genuine writings could not recognize those others as mine; although by other persons my authorship of them was quite believed.

Chapter 20. —The Same Continued. Pelagius Acknowledges the Doctrine of Grace in Deceptive Terms.

There can be no doubt that what Pelagius has acknowledged as his own is as yet very obscure. I suppose, however, that it will become apparent in the subsequent details of these proceedings. Now he says: "We have affirmed that a man is able to be without sin, and to keep the commandments of God if he wishes, inasmuch as God has given him this ability. But we have not said that any man can be found, who from infancy to old age has never committed sin; but that if any person were converted from his sins, he could by his own exertion and God's grace be without sin; and yet not even thus would he be incapable of change afterwards." Now it is quite uncertain what he means in these words by the grace of God; and the judges, catholic as they were, could not possibly understand by the phrase anything else than the grace which is so very strongly recommended to us in the apostle's teaching. Now this is the grace whereby we hope that we can be delivered from the body of this death through our Lord Jesus Christ, [VII.] and for the obtaining of which we pray that we may not be led into temptation. This grace is not nature, but that which renders assistance to frail and corrupted nature. This grace is not the knowledge of the law, but is that of which the apostle says: "I will not make void the grace of God: for if righteousness come by the law, then Christ is dead in vain." Therefore it is not "the letter that kills, but the life-giving spirit." For the knowledge of the law, without the grace of the Spirit, produces all kinds of concupiscence in man; for, as the apostle says, "I had not known sin but by the law: I had not known lust, unless the law had said, Thou shalt not covet. But sin, taking occasion by the commandment, wrought in me all manner of concupiscence." By saying this, however, he blames not the law; he rather praises it, for he says afterwards: "The law indeed is holy, and the commandment holy, and just, and good." And he goes on to ask: "Was then that which is good made death unto me? God forbid. But sin, that it might appear sin, wrought death in me by that which is good." And, again, he praises the law by saying: "We know that the law is spiritual; but I am carnal, sold under sin. For that which I do I know not: for what I would, that do I not; but what I hate, that do I. If then I do that which I would not, I consent unto the law that it is good." Observe, then, he knows the law, praises it, and consents to it; for what it commands, that he also wishes; and what it forbids, and condemns, that he also hates: but for all that, what he hates, that he actually does. There is in his mind, therefore, a knowledge of the holy law of God, but still his evil concupiscence is not cured. He has a good will within him, but still what he does is evil. Hence it comes to pass that, amidst the mutual struggles of the two laws within him, — "the law in his members warring against the law of his mind, and making him captive to the law of sin,"—he confesses his misery; and exclaims in such words as these: "O wretched man that I am! who shall deliver me from this body of death? The grace of God, through Jesus Christ our Lord."

Chapter 21 [VIII.]—The Same Continued.

It is not nature, therefore, which, sold as it is under sin and wounded by the offence, longs for a Redeemer and Savior; nor is it the knowledge of the law—through which comes the discovery, not the expulsion, of sin—which delivers us from the body of this death; but it is the Lord's good grace through our Lord Jesus Christ.

Chapter 21 [IX.]—The Same Continued.

This grace is not dying nature, nor the slaying letter, but the vivifying spirit; for already did he possess nature with freedom of will, because he said: "To will is present with me." Nature, however, in a healthy condition and without a flaw, he did not possess, for he said: "I know that in me (that is, in my flesh) dwelleth nothing good." Already had he the knowledge of God's holy law, for he said: "I had not known sin but through the law;" yet for all that, he did not possess strength and power to practice and fulfil righteousness, for he complained: "What I would, that do I not; but what I hate, that do I." And again, "How to accomplish that which is good I find not." Therefore, it is not from the liberty of the human will, nor from the precepts of the law, that there comes deliverance from the body of this death; for both of these he had already, —the one in his nature, the other in his learning; but all he wanted was the help of the grace of God, through Jesus Christ our Lord.

Chapter 22 [X.]—The Same Continued. The Synod Supposed that the Grace Acknowledged by Pelagius Was that Which Was So Thoroughly Known to the Church.

This grace, then, which was most completely known in the catholic Church (as the bishops were well aware), they supposed Pelagius made confession of, when they heard him say that "a man, when converted from his sins, is able by his own exertion and the grace of God to be without sin." For my own part, however, I remembered the treatise which had been given to me, that I might refute it, by those servants of God, who had been Pelagius' followers. They, notwithstanding their great affection for him, plainly acknowledged that the passage was his; when, on this question being proposed, because he had already given offence to very many persons from advancing views against the grace of God, he most expressly admitted that "what he meant by God's grace was that, when our nature was created, it received the capacity of not sinning, because it was created with free will." On account, therefore, of this treatise, I cannot help feeling still anxious, whilst many of the brethren who are well acquainted with his discussions, share in my anxiety, lest under the ambiguity which notoriously characterizes his words there lies some latent reserve, and lest he should afterwards tell his followers that it was without prejudice to his own doctrine that he made any admissions,—discoursing thus: "I no doubt asserted that a man was able by his own exertion and the grace of God to live without sin; but you know very well what I mean by grace; and you may recollect reading that grace is that in which we are created by God with a free will." Accordingly, while the bishops understood him to mean the grace by which we have by adoption been made new creatures, not that by which we were created (for most plainly does Holy Scripture instruct us in the former sense of grace as the true one), ignorant of his being a heretic, they acquitted him as a catholic. I must say that my suspicion is excited also by this, that in the work which I answered, he most openly said that "righteous Abel never sinned at all." Now, however, he thus expresses himself: "But we did not say that any man could be found who at no time whatever, from infancy to old age, has committed sin; but that, if any man were converted from his sins, he could by his own labor and God's grace be without sin." When speaking of righteous Abel, he did not say that after being converted from his sins he became sinless in a new life, but that he never committed sin at all. If, then, that book be his, it must of course be corrected and amended from his answer. For I should be sorry to say that he was insincere in his more recent statement; lest perhaps he should say that he had forgotten what he had previously written in the book we have quoted. Let us therefore direct our view to what afterwards occurred. Now, from the sequel of these ecclesiastical proceedings, we can by God's help show that, although Pelagius, as some suppose, cleared himself in his examination, and was at all events acquitted by his judges (who were, however, but human beings after all), that this great heresy, which we should be most unwilling to see making further progress or becoming aggravated in guilt, was undoubtedly itself condemned.

Chapter 23 [XI.]—The Seventh Item of the Accusation: the Breviates of Cœlestius Objected to Pelagius.

Then follow sundry statements charged against Pelagius, which are said to be found among the opinions of his disciple Cœlestius: how that "Adam was created mortal, and would have died whether he had sinned or not sinned; that Adam's sin injured only himself and not the human race; that the law no less than the gospel leads us to the kingdom; that there were sinless men previous to the coming of Christ; that new-born infants are in the same condition as Adam was before the fall; that the whole human race does not, on the one hand, die through Adam's death or transgression, nor, on the other hand, does the whole human race rise again through the resurrection of Christ." These have been so objected to, that they are even said to have been, after a full hearing, condemned at Carthage by your holiness and other bishops associated with you. I was not present on that occasion, as you will recollect; but afterwards, on my arrival at Carthage, I read over the Acts of the synod, some of which I perfectly well remember, but I do not know whether all the tenets now mentioned occur among them. But what matters it if some of them were possibly not mentioned, and so not included in the condemnation of the synod when it is quite clear that they deserve condemnation? Sundry other points of error were next alleged against him, connected with the mention of my own name. They had been transmitted to me from Sicily, some of our Catholic brethren there being perplexed by questions of this kind; and I drew up a reply to them in a little work addressed to Hilary, who had consulted me respecting them in a letter. My answer, in my opinion, was a sufficient one. These are the errors referred to: "That a man is able to be without sin if he wishes. That infants, even if they die unbaptized, have eternal life. That rich men, even if they are baptized, unless they renounce all, have, whatever good they may seem to have done, nothing of it reckoned to them; neither can they possess the kingdom of God."

Chapter 24. —Pelagius' Answer to the Charges Brought Together Under the Seventh Item.

The following, as the proceedings testify, was

Pelagius' own answer to these charges against him: "Concerning a man's being able indeed to be without sin, we have spoken," says he, "already; concerning the fact, however, that before the Lord's coming there were persons without sin, we say now that, previous to Christ's advent, some men lived holy and righteous lives, according to the teaching of the sacred Scriptures. The rest were not said by me, as even their testimony goes to show, and for them, I do not feel that I am responsible. But for the satisfaction of the holy synod, I anathematize those who either now hold, or have ever held, these opinions." After hearing this answer of his, the synod said: "With regard to these charges aforesaid, Pelagius has in our presence given us sufficient and proper satisfaction, by anathematizing the opinions which were not his." We see, therefore, and maintain that the most pernicious evils of this heresy have been condemned, not only by Pelagius, but also by the holy bishops who presided over that inquiry:—that "Adam was made mortal;" (and, that the meaning of this statement might be more clearly understood, it was added, "and he would have died whether he had sinned or not sinned;") that his sin injured only himself and not the human race; that the law, no less than the gospel, leads us to the kingdom of heaven; that new born infants are in the same condition that Adam was before the fall; that the entire human race does not, on the one hand, die through Adam's death and transgression, nor, on the other hand, does the whole human race rise again through the resurrection of Christ; that infants, even if they die unbaptized, have eternal life; that rich men even if baptized, unless they renounce and give up all, have, whatever good they may seem to have done, nothing of it reckoned to them, neither can they possess the kingdom of God;"—all these opinions, at any rate, were clearly condemned in that ecclesiastical court,—Pelagius pronouncing the anathema, and the bishops the interlocutory sentence.

Chapter 25. —The Pelagians Falsely Pretended that the Eastern Churches Were on Their Side.

Now, because of these questions, and the very contentious assertions of these tenets, which are everywhere accompanied with heated feelings, many weak brethren were disturbed. We have accordingly, in the anxiety of that love which it becomes us to feel towards the Church of Christ through His grace, and out of regard to Marcellinus of blessed memory (who was extremely vexed day by day by these disputers, and who asked my advice by letter), been obliged to write on some of these questions, and especially on the baptism of infants. On this same subject also I afterwards, at your request, and assisted by your prayers, delivered an earnest address, to the best of my ability, in the church of the Majores, holding in my hands an epistle of the most glorious martyr Cyprian, and reading therefrom and applying his words on the very matter, in order to remove this dangerous error out of the hearts of sundry persons, who had been persuaded to take up with the opinions which, as we see, were condemned in these proceedings. These opinions it has been attempted by their promoters to force upon the minds of some of the brethren, by threatening, as if from the Eastern Churches, that unless they adopted the said opinions, they would be formally condemned by those Churches. Observe, however, that no less than fourteen bishops of the Eastern Church, assembled in synod in the land where the Lord manifested His presence in the days of His flesh, refused to acquit Pelagius unless he condemned these opinions as opposed to the Catholic faith. Since, therefore, he was then acquitted because he anathematized such views, it follows beyond a doubt that the said opinions were condemned. This, indeed, will appear more clearly still, and on still stronger evidence, in the sequel.

Chapter 26. —The Accusations in the Seventh Item, Which Pelagius Confessed.

Let us now see what were the two points out of all that were alleged which Pelagius was unwilling to anathematize, and admitted being his own opinions, but to remove their offensive aspect explained in what sense he held them. "That a man," says he, "is able to be without sin has been asserted already." Asserted no doubt, and we remember the assertion quite well; but still it was mitigated, and approved by the judges, in that God's grace was added, concerning which nothing was said in the original draft of his doctrine. Touching the second, however, of these points, we ought to pay careful attention to what he said in answer to the charge against him. "Concerning the fact, indeed," says he, "that before the Lord's coming there were persons without sin, we now again assert that before Christ's advent some men lived holy and righteous lives, according to the teaching of the sacred Scriptures." He did not dare to say: "We now again assert that before Christ's advent there were persons without sin," although this had been laid to his charge after the very words of Cœlestius. For he perceived how dangerous such a statement was, and into what trouble it would bring him. So he reduced the sentence to these harmless dimensions: "We again assert that before the coming of Christ there were persons who led holy and righteous lives." Of course there were: who would deny it? But to say this is a very different thing from saying that they lived "without sin." Because, indeed, those ancient worthies lived holy and righteous lives, they could for that very reason better confess: "If we say that we have no sin, we deceive ourselves, and the truth is not in us." In the present day, also, many men live holy and righteous lives; but yet it is no untruth they utter when in their prayer they say: "Forgive us our debts, even as we forgive our debtors." This avowal was accordingly acceptable to the judges, in the sense in which Pelagius solemnly declared his belief; but certainly not in the sense which Cœlestius, according to the original charge against him, was said to hold. We must now treat in detail of the topics which still remain, to the best of our ability.

Chapter 27 [XII.]—The Eighth Item in the Accusation.

Pelagius was charged with having said: "That the Church here is without spot or wrinkle." It was on this point that the Donatists also were constantly at conflict with us in our conference. We used, in their case, to lay especial stress on the mixture of bad men with good, like that of the chaff with the wheat; and we were led to this idea by the similitude of the threshing-floor. We might apply the same illustration in answer to our present opponents, unless indeed they would have the Church consist only of good men, whom they assert to be without any sin whatever, that so the Church might be without spot or wrinkle. If this be their meaning, then I repeat the same words as I quoted just now; for how can they be members of the Church, of whom the voice of a truthful humility declares, "If we say that we have no sin, we deceive ourselves, and the truth is not in us?" or how could the Church offer up that prayer which the Lord taught her to use, "Forgive us our debts," if in this world the Church is without a spot or blemish? In short, they must themselves submit to be strictly catechized respecting themselves: do they really allow that they have any sins of their own? If their answer is in the negative, then they must be plainly told that they are deceiving themselves, and the truth is not in them. If, however, they shall acknowledge that they do commit sin, what is this but a confession of their own wrinkle and spot? They therefore are not members of the Church; because the Church is without spot and wrinkle, while they have both spot and wrinkle.

Chapter 28. —Pelagius' Reply to the Eighth Item of Accusation.

But to this objection he replied with a watchful caution such as the catholic judges no doubt approved. "It has," says he, "been asserted by me, —but in such a sense that the Church is by the laver cleansed from every spot and wrinkle, and in this purity the Lord wishes her to continue." Whereupon the synod said: "Of this also we approve." And who amongst us denies that in baptism the sins of all men are remitted, and that all believers come up spotless and pure from the laver of regeneration? Or what catholic Christian is there who wishes not, as his Lord also wishes, and as it is meant to be, that the Church should remain always without spot or wrinkle? For in very deed God is now in His mercy and truth bringing it about, that His Holy Church should be conducted to that perfect state in which she is to remain without spot or wrinkle for evermore. But between the laver, where all past stains and deformities are removed, and the kingdom, where the Church will remain forever without any spot or wrinkle, there is this present intermediate time of prayer, during which her cry must of necessity be: "Forgive us our debts." Hence arose the objection against them for saying that "the Church here on earth is without spot or wrinkle;" from the doubt whether by this opinion they did not boldly prohibit that prayer whereby the Church in her present baptized state entreats day and night for herself the forgiveness of her sins. About this intervening period between the remission of sins which takes place in baptism, and the perpetuity of sinlessness which is to be in the kingdom of heaven, no proceedings ensued with Pelagius, and no decision was pronounced by the bishops. Only he thought that some brief indication ought to be given that he had not expressed himself in the way which the accusation against him seemed to state. As to his saying, "This has been asserted by me, —but in such a sense," what else did he mean to convey than the idea that he had not in fact expressed himself in the same manner as he was supposed to have done by his accusers? That, however, which induced the judges to say that they were satisfied with his answer was baptism as the means of being washed from our sins; and the kingdom of heaven, in which the holy Church, which is now in process of cleansing, shall continue in a sinless state forever: this is clear from the evidence, so far as I can form an opinion.

Chapter 29 [XIII.]—The Ninth Item of the Accusation; And Pelagius' Reply.

The next objections were urged out of the book of Cœlestius, following the contents of each several chapter, but rather according to the sense than the words. These indeed he expatiates on rather fully; they, however, who presented the indictment against Pelagius said that they had been unable at the moment to adduce all the words. In the first chapter, then, of Cœlestius' book they alleged that the following was written: "That we do more than is commanded us in the law and the gospel." To this Pelagius replied: "This they have set down as my statement. What we said, however, was in keeping with the apostle's assertion concerning virginity, of which Paul writes: 'I have no commandment of the Lord.'" Upon this the synod said: "This also the Church receives." I have read for myself the meaning which Cœlestius gives to this in his book, —for he does not deny that the book is his. Now he made this statement obviously with the view of persuading us that we possess through the nature of free will so great an ability for avoiding sin, that we are able to do more than is commanded us; for a perpetual virginity is maintained by very many persons, and this is not commanded; whereas, in order to avoid sin, it is sufficient to fulfil what is commanded. When the judges, however, accepted Pelagius' answer, they did not take it to convey the idea that those persons keep all the commandments of the law and the gospel who over and above maintain the state of virginity, which is not commanded,—but only this, that virginity, which is not commanded, is something more than conjugal chastity, which is commanded; so that to observe the one is of course more than to keep the other; whereas, at the same time, neither can be maintained without the grace of God, inasmuch as the apostle, in speaking of this very subject, says: "But I would that all men were even as I myself. Every man, however, hath his proper gift of God, one after this manner, and another after that." And even the Lord Himself, upon the disciples remarking, "If the case of the man be so with his wife, it is not expedient to marry" (or, as it may be better expressed in Latin, "it is not expedient to take a wife"), said to them: "All men cannot receive this saying, save they to whom it is given." This, therefore, is the doctrine which the bishops of the synod declared to be received by the Church, that the state of virginity, persevered in to the last, which is not commanded, is more than the chastity of married life, which is commanded. In what view Pelagius or Cœlestius regarded this subject, the judges were not aware.

Chapter 30 [XIV.]—The Tenth Item in the Accusation. The More Prominent Points of Cœlestius' Work Continued. After this we find objected against Pelagius some other points of Cœlestius' teaching, — prominent ones, and undoubtedly worthy of condemnation; such, indeed, as would certainly have involved Pelagius in condemnation, if he had not anathematized them in the synod. Under his third head Cœlestius was alleged to have written: "That God's grace and assistance is not given for single actions, but is imparted in the freedom of the will, or in the law and in doctrine." And again: "That God's grace is given in proportion to our deserts; because, were He to give it to sinful persons, He would seem to be unrighteous." And from these words he inferred that "therefore grace itself has been placed in my will, according as I have been either worthy or unworthy of it. For if we do all things by grace, then whenever we are overcome by sin, it is not we who are overcome, but God's grace, which wanted by all means to help us, but was not able." And once more he says: "If, when we conquer sin, it is by the grace of God; then it is He who is in fault whenever we are conquered by sin, because He was either altogether unable or unwilling to keep us safe." To these charges Pelagius replied: "Whether these are really the opinions of Cœlestius or not, is the concern of those who say that they are. For my own part, indeed, I never entertained such views; on the contrary, I anathematize everyone who does entertain them." Then the synod said: "This holy synod accepts you for your condemnation of these impious words." Now certainly there can be no mistake, regarding these opinions, either as to the clear way in which Pelagius pronounced on them his anathema, or as to the absolute terms in which the bishops condemned them. Whether Pelagius or Cœlestius, or both of them, or neither of them, or other persons with them or in their name, have ever held or still hold these sentiments, — may be doubtful or obscure; but nevertheless, by this judgment of the bishops it has been declared plainly enough that they have been condemned, and that Pelagius would have been condemned along with them, unless he had himself condemned them too. Now, after this trial, it is certain that whenever we enter on a controversy touching opinions of this kind, we only discuss an already condemned heresy.

Chapter 31. —Remarks on the Tenth Item.

I shall make my next remark with greater satisfaction. In a former section I expressed a fear that, when Pelagius said that "a man was able by the help of God's grace to live without sin," he perhaps meant by the term "grace" the capability possessed by nature as created by God with a free will, as it is understood in that book which I received as his and to which I replied; and that by these means he was deceiving the judges, who were ignorant of the circumstances. Now, however, since he anathematizes those persons who hold that "God's grace and assistance is not given for single actions, but is imparted in the freedom of the will, or in the law and in doctrine," it is quite evident that he really means the grace which is preached in the Church of Christ, and is conferred by the ministration of the Holy Ghost for the purpose of helping us in our single actions, whence it is that we pray for needful and suitable grace that we enter not into any temptation. Nor, again, have I any longer a fear that, when he said, "No man can be without sin unless he has acquired a knowledge of the law," and added this explanation of his words, that "he posited in the knowledge of the law, help towards the avoidance of sin," he at all meant the said knowledge to be considered as tantamount to the grace of God; for, observe, he anathematizes such as hold this opinion. See, too, how he refuses to hold our natural free will, or the law and doctrine, as equivalent to that grace of God which helps us through our single actions. What else then is left to him but to understand that grace which the apostle tells us is given by "the supply of the Spirit?" and concerning which the Lord said: "Take no thought how or what ye shall speak; for it shall be given you in that same hour what ye shall speak. For it is not ye that speak, but the Spirit of your Father which speaks in you." Nor, again, need I be under any apprehension that, when he asserted, "All men are ruled by their own will," and afterwards explained that he had made that statement "in the interest of the freedom of our will, of which God is the helper whenever it makes choice of good," that he perhaps here also held God's helping grace as synonymous with our natural free will and the teaching of the law. For inasmuch as he rightly anathematized the persons who hold that God's grace or assistance is not given for single actions, but lies in the gift of free will, or in the law and doctrine, it follows, of course, that God's grace or assistance is given us for single actions,—free will, or the law and the doctrine, being left out of consideration; and thus through all the single actions of our life, when we act rightly, we are ruled and directed by God; nor is our prayer a useless one, wherein we say: "Order my steps according to Thy word, and let not any iniquity have dominion over me."

Chapter 32. —The Eleventh Item of the Accusation.

But what comes afterwards again fills me with anxiety. On its being objected to him, from the fifth chapter of Cœlestius' book, that "they say that every individual can possess all powers and graces, thus taking away that 'diversity of graces,' which the apostle teaches," Pelagius replied: "We have certainly said so much; but yet they have laid against us a malignant and blundering charge. We do not take away the diversity of graces; but we declare that God gives to the person, who has proved himself worthy to receive them, all graces, even as He conferred them on the Apostle Paul." Hereupon the Synod said: "You accordingly do yourself hold the doctrine of the Church touching the gift of the graces, which are collectively possessed by the apostle." Here someone may say, "Why then is he anxious? Do you on your side deny that all the powers and graces were combined in the apostle?" For my own part, indeed, if all those are to be understood which the apostle has himself mentioned together in one passage,—as, I suppose, the bishops understood Pelagius to mean when they approved of his answer, and pronounced it to be in keeping with the sense of the Church,—then I do not doubt that the apostle had them all; for he says: "And God hath set some in the Church, first, apostles; secondarily, prophets; thirdly, teachers; after that miracles; then gifts of healings, helps, governments, diversities of tongues." What then? shall we say that the Apostle Paul did not possess all these gifts himself? Who would be bold enough to assert this? The very fact that he was an apostle showed, of course, that he possessed the grace of the apostolate. He possessed also that of prophecy; for was not that a prophecy of his in which he says: "In the last times some shall depart from the faith, giving heed to seducing spirits, and doctrines of devils?" He was, moreover, "the teacher of the Gentiles in faith and verity." He performed miracles also and cures; for he shook off from his hand, unhurt, the biting viper; and the cripple stood upright on his feet at the apostle's word, and his strength was at once restored. It is not clear what he means by helps, for the term is of very wide application; but who can say that he was wanting even in this grace, when through his labors such helps were manifestly afforded towards the salvation of mankind?

Then as to his possessing the grace of "government," what could be more excellent than his administration, when the Lord at that time governed so many churches by his personal agency, and governs them still in our day through his epistles? And in respect of the "diversities of tongues," what tongues could have been wanting to him, when he says himself: "I thank my God that I speak with tongues more than you all?" It being thus inevitable to suppose that not one of these was wanting to the Apostle Paul, the judges approved of Pelagius' answer, wherein he said "that all graces were conferred upon him." But there are other graces in addition to these which are not mentioned here. For it is not to be supposed, however greatly the Apostle Paul excelled others as a member of Christ's body, that the very Head itself of the entire body did not receive more and ampler graces still, whether in His flesh or His soul as man; for such a created nature did the Word of God assume as His own into the unity of His Person, that He might be our Head, and we His body. And in very deed, if all gifts could be in each member, it would be evident that the similitude, which is used to illustrate this subject, of the several members of our body is inapplicable; for some things are common to the members in general, such as life and health, whilst other things are peculiar to the separate members, since the ear has no perception of colors, nor the eye of voices. Hence it is written: "If the whole body were an eye, where were the hearing? if the whole were hearing, where were the smelling?" Now this of course is not said as if it were impossible for God to impart to the ear the sense of seeing, or to the eye the function of hearing. However, what He does in Christ's body, which is the Church, and what the apostle meant by diversity of graces as if through the different members, there might be gifts proper even to everyone separately, is clearly known. Why, too, and on what ground they who raised the objection were so unwilling to have taken away all difference in graces, why, moreover, the bishops of the synod were able to approve of the answer given by Pelagius in deference to the Apostle Paul, in whom we admit the combination of all those graces which he mentioned in the one particular passage, is by this time clear also.

Chapter 33. —Discussion of the Eleventh Item Continued.

What, then, is the reason why, as I said just now, I felt anxious about this head of his doctrine? It is occasioned by what Pelagius says in these words: "That God gives to the man who has proved himself worthy to receive them, all graces, even as He conferred them on the Apostle Paul." Now, I should not have felt any anxiety about this answer of Pelagius, if it were not closely connected with the cause which we are bound to guard with the utmost care—even that God's grace may never be attacked, while we are silent or dissembling in respect of so great an evil. As, therefore, he does not say, that God gives to whom He will, but that "God gives to the man who has proved himself worthy to receive them, all these graces," I could not help being suspicious, when I read such words. For the very name of grace, and the thing that is meant by it, is taken away, if it is not bestowed gratuitously, but he only receives it who is worthy of it. Will anybody say that I do the apostle wrong, because I do not admit him to have been worthy of grace? Nay, I should indeed rather do him wrong, and bring on myself a punishment, if I refused to believe what he himself says. Well, now, has he not pointedly so defined grace as to show that it is so called because it is bestowed gratuitously? These are his own very words: "And if by grace, then is it no more of works; otherwise grace is no more grace." In accordance with this, he says again: "Now to him that worketh is the reward not reckoned of grace, but of debt." Whosoever, therefore, is worthy, to him it is due; and if it is thus due to him, it ceases to be grace; for grace is given, but a debt is paid. Grace, therefore, is given to those who are unworthy, that a debt may be paid to them when they become worthy. He, however, who has bestowed on the unworthy the gifts which they possessed not before, does Himself take care that they shall have whatever things He means to recompense to them when they become worthy.

Chapter 34. —The Same Continued. On the Works of Unbelievers; Faith is the Initial Principle from Which Good Works Have Their Beginning; Faith is the Gift of God's Grace.

He will perhaps say to this: "It was not because of his works, but in consequence of his faith, that I said the apostle was worthy of having all those great graces bestowed upon him. His faith deserved this distinction, but not his works, which were not previously good." Well, then, are we to suppose that faith does not work? Surely faith does work in a very real way, for it "worketh by love." Preach up, however, as much as you like, the works of unbelieving men, we still know how true and invincible is the statement of this same apostle: "Whatsoever is not of faith is sin." The very reason, indeed, why he so often declares that righteousness is imputed to us, not out of our works, but our faith, whereas faith rather works through love, is that no man should think that he arrives at faith itself through the merit of his works; for it is faith which is the beginning whence good works first proceed; since (as has already been stated) whatsoever comes not from faith is sin. Accordingly, it is said to the Church, in the Song of Songs: "Thou shalt come and pass by from the beginning of faith." Although, therefore, faith procures the grace of producing good works, we certainly do not deserve by any faith that we should have faith itself; but, in its bestowal upon us, in order that we may follow the Lord by its help, "His mercy has prevented us." Was it we ourselves that gave it to us? Did we ourselves make ourselves faithful? I must by all means say here, emphatically: "It is He that hath made us, and not we ourselves." And indeed, nothing else than this is pressed upon us in the apostle's teaching, when he says: "For I declare, through the grace that is given unto me, to every man that is among you, not to think of himself more highly than he ought to think; but to think soberly, according as God hath dealt to every man the measure of faith." Whence, too, arises the well-known challenge: "What hast thou that thou didst not receive?" inasmuch as we have received even that which is the spring from which everything we have of good in our actions takes its beginning.

Chapter 35. —The Same Continued.

"What, then, is the meaning of that which the same apostle says: 'I have fought a good fight, I have finished my course, I have kept the faith: henceforth there is laid up for me a crown of righteousness, which the Lord, the righteous judge, shall give me at that day;' if these are not recompenses paid to the worthy, but gifts, bestowed on the unworthy?" He who says this, does not consider that the crown could not have been given to the man who is worthy of it, unless grace had been first bestowed on him whilst unworthy of it. He says indeed: "I have fought a good fight;" but then he also says: "Thanks be to God, who giveth us the victory through Jesus Christ our Lord." He says too: "I have finished my course;" but he says again: "It is not of him that wills, nor of him that runs, but of God that shows mercy." He says, moreover: "I have kept the faith;" but then it is he too who says again: "I know whom I have believed, and am persuaded that He is able to keep my deposit against that day"—that is, "my commendation;" for some copies have not the word depositum, but commendatum, which yields a plainer sense. Now, what do we commend to God's keeping, except the things which we pray Him to preserve for us, and amongst these our very faith? For what else did the Lord procure for the Apostle Peter by His prayer for him, of which He said, "I have prayed for thee, Peter, that thy faith fail not," than that God would preserve his faith, that it should not fail by giving way to temptation? Therefore, blessed Paul, thou great preacher of grace, I will say it without fear of any man (for who will be less angry with me for so saying than thyself, who hast told us what to say, and taught us what to teach?)—I will, I repeat, say it, and fear no man for the assertion: Their own crown is recompensed to their merits; but thy merits are the gifts of God!

Chapter 36. —The Same Continued. The Monk Pelagius. Grace is Conferred on the Unworthy.

His due reward, therefore, is recompensed to the apostle as worthy of it; but still it was grace which bestowed on him the apostleship itself, which was not his due, and of which he was not worthy. Shall I be sorry for having said this? God forbid! For under his own testimony shall I find a ready protection from such reproach; nor will any man charge me with audacity, unless he be himself audacious enough to charge the apostle with mendacity. He frankly says, nay he protests, that he commends the gifts of God within himself, so that he glories not in himself at all, but in the Lord; he not only declares that he possessed no good deserts in himself why he should be made an apostle, but he even mentions his own demerits, in order to manifest and preach the grace of God. "I am not meet," says he, "to be called an apostle;" and what else does this mean than "I am not worthy"—as indeed several Latin copies read the phrase. Now this, to be sure, is the very gist of our question; for undoubtedly in this grace of apostleship all those graces are contained. For it was neither convenient nor right that an apostle should not possess the gift of prophecy, nor be a teacher, nor be illustrious for miracles and the gifts of healings, nor furnish needful helps, nor provide governments over the churches, nor excel in diversities of tongues. All these functions the one name of apostleship embraces. Let us, therefore, consult the man himself, nay listen wholly to him. Let us say to him: "Holy Apostle Paul, the monk Pelagius declares that thou was worthy to receive all the graces of thine apostleship. What dost thou say thyself?" He answers: "I am not worthy to be called an apostle." Shall I then, under pretense of honoring Paul, in a matter concerning Paul, dare to believe Pelagius in preference to Paul? I will not do so; for if I did, I should only prove to be more onerous to myself than honoring to him. Let us hear also why he is not worthy to be called an apostle: "Because," says he, "I persecuted the Church of God." Now, were we to follow up the idea here expressed, who would not judge that he rather deserved from Christ condemnation, instead of an apostolic call? Who could so love the preacher as not to loathe the persecutor? Well, therefore, and truly does he say of himself: "I am not worthy to be called an apostle, because I persecuted the Church of God." As thou wrought then such evil, how came to earn such good? Let all men hear his answer: "But by the grace of God, I am what I am." Is there, then, no other way in which grace is commended, than because it is conferred on an unworthy recipient? "And His grace," he adds, "which was bestowed on me was not in vain." He says this as a lesson to others also, to show the freedom of the will, when he says: "We then, as workers together with Him, beseech you also that ye receive not the grace of God in vain." Whence however does he derive his proof, that "His grace bestowed on himself was not in vain," except from the fact which he goes on to mention: "But I labored more abundantly than they all?" So, it seems he did not labor in order to receive grace, but he received grace in order that he might labor. And thus, when unworthy, he gratuitously received grace, whereby he might become worthy to receive the due reward. Not that he ventured to claim even his labor for himself; for, after saying: "I labored more abundantly than they all," he at once subjoined: "Yet not I, but the grace of God which was with me." O mighty teacher, confessor, and preacher of grace! What meant this: "I labored more, yet not I?" Where the will exalted itself ever so little, there piety was instantly on the watch, and humility trembled, because weakness recognized itself.

Chapter 37—The Same Continued. John, Bishop of Jerusalem, and His Examination.

With great propriety, as the proceedings show, did John, the holy overseer of the Church of Jerusalem, employ the authority of this same passage of the apostle, as he himself told our brethren the bishops who were his assessors at that trial, on their asking him what proceedings had taken place before him previous to the trial. He told them that "on the occasion in question, whilst some were whispering, and remarking on Pelagius' statement, that 'without God's grace man was able to attain perfection' (that is, as he had previously expressed it, 'man was able to be without sin'), he censured the statement, and reminded them besides, that even the Apostle Paul, after so many labors—not indeed in his own strength, but by the grace of God—said: 'I labored more abundantly than they all: yet not I, but the grace of God that was with me;' and again: 'It is not of him that wills, nor of him that runs, but of God that shows mercy;' and again: 'Except the Lord build the house, they labor but in vain who build it.' And," he added, "we quoted several other like passages out of the Holy Scriptures. When, however, they did not receive the quotations which we made out of the Holy Scriptures, but continued their murmuring noise, Pelagius said: 'This is what I also believe; let him be anathema, who declares that a man is able, without God's help, to arrive at the perfection of all virtues.'"

Chapter 38 [XV.]—The Same Continued.

Bishop John narrated all this in the hearing of Pelagius; but he, of course, might respectfully say: "Your holiness is in error; you do not accurately remember the facts. It was not about the passages of Scripture which you have quoted that I uttered the words: 'This is what I also believe.' Because this is not my opinion of them. I do not understand them to say, that God's grace so co-operates with man, that his abstinence from sin is due, not to 'him that wills, nor to him that runs, but to God that shows mercy.'"

Chapter 39 [XVI.]—The Same Continued. Heros and Lazarus; Orosius.

Now there are some expositions of Paul's Epistle to the Romans which are said to have been written by Pelagius himself, —in which he asserts, that the passage: "Not of him that wills, nor of him that runs, but of God that shows mercy," was "not said in Paul's own person; but that he therein employed the language of questioning and refutation, as if such a statement ought not to be made." No safe conclusion, therefore, can be drawn, although the bishop John plainly acknowledged the passage in question as conveying the mind of the apostle, and mentioned it for the very purpose of hindering Pelagius from thinking that any man can avoid sin without God's grace, and declared that Pelagius said in answer: "This is what I also believe," and did not, upon hearing all this, repudiate his admission by replying:

"This is not my belief." He ought, indeed, either to deny altogether, or unhesitatingly to correct and amend this perverse exposition, in which he would have it, that the apostle must not be regarded as entertaining the sentiment, but rather as refuting it. Now, whatever Bishop John said of our brethren who were absent—whether our brother bishops Heros and Lazarus, or the presbyter Orosius, or any others whose names are not there registered, —I am sure that he did not mean it to operate to their prejudice. For, had they been present, they might possibly (I am far from saying it absolutely) have convicted him of untruth; at any rate they might perhaps have reminded him of something he had forgotten, or something in which he might have been deceived by the Latin interpreter—not, to be sure, for the purpose of misleading him by untruth, but at least, owing to some difficulty occasioned by a foreign language, only imperfectly understood; especially as the question was not treated in the Proceedings, which were drawn up for the useful purpose of preventing deceit on the part of evil men, and of preserving a record to assist the memory of good men. If, however, any man shall be disposed by this mention of our brethren to introduce any question or doubt on the subject, and summon them before the Episcopal judgment, they will not be wanting to themselves, as occasion shall serve. Why need we here pursue the point, when not even the judges themselves, after the narrative of our brother bishop, were inclined to pronounce any definite sentence in consequence of it?

Chapter 40 [XVII.]—The Same Continued.

Since, then, Pelagius was present when these passages of the Scriptures were discussed, and by his silence acknowledged having said that he entertained the same view of their meaning, how happens it, that, after reconsidering the apostle's testimony, as he had just done, and finding that he said: "I am not meet to be called an apostle, because I persecuted the Church of God; but by the grace of God I am what I am," he did not perceive that it was improper for him to say, respecting the question of the abundance of the graces which the said apostle received, that he had shown himself "worthy to receive them," when the apostle himself not only confessed, but added a reason to prove, that he was unworthy of them—and by this very fact set forth grace as grace indeed? If he could not for some reason or other consider or recollect the narrative of his holiness the bishop John, which he had heard some time before, he might surely have respected his own very recent answer at the synod, and remembered how he anathematized, but a short while before, the opinions which had been alleged against him out of Cœlestius. Now among these it was objected to him that Cœlestius had said: "That the grace of God is bestowed according to our merits." If, then, Pelagius truthfully anathematized this, why does he say that all those graces were conferred on the apostle because he deserved them? Is the phrase "worthy to receive" of different meaning from the expression "to receive according to merit"? Can he by any disputatious subtlety show that a man is worthy who has no merit? But neither Cœlestius, nor any other, all of whose opinions he anathematized, has any intention to allow him to throw clouds over the phrase, and to conceal himself behind them. He presses home the matter, and plainly says: "And this grace has been placed in my will, according as I have been either worthy or unworthy of it." If, then, a statement, wherein it is declared that "God's grace is given in proportion to our deserts, to such as are worthy," was rightly and truly condemned by Pelagius, how could his heart permit him to think, or his mouth to utter, such a sentence as this: "We say that God gives to the person who has proved himself worthy to receive them, all graces?" Who that carefully considers all this can help feeling some anxiety about his answer or defense?

Chapter 41. —Augustin Indulgently Shows that the Judges Acted Incautiously in Their Official Conduct of the Case of Pelagius.

Why, then (someone will say), did the judges approve of this? I confess that I hardly even now understand why they did. It is, however, not to be wondered at, if some brief word or phrase too easily escaped their attention and ear; or if, because they thought it capable of being somehow interpreted in a correct sense, from seeming to have from the accused himself such clear confessions of truth on the subject, they decided it to be hardly worthwhile to excite a discussion about a word. The same feeling might have occurred to ourselves also, if we had sat with them at the trial. For if, instead of the term worthy, the word predestinated had been used, or some such word, my mind would certainly not have entertained any doubt, much less have been disquieted by it; and yet if it were asserted, that he who is justified by the election of grace is called worthy, through no antecedent merits of good indeed, but by destination, just as he is called "elect," it would be really difficult to determine whether he might be so designated at all, or at least without some offence to an intelligent view of the subject.

As for myself, indeed, I might readily pass on from the discussion on this word, were it not that the treatise which called forth my reply, and in which he says that there is no God's grace at all except our own nature gratuitously created with free will, made me suspicious and anxious about the actual meaning of Pelagius—whether he had procured the introduction of the term into the argument without any accurate intention as to its sense, or else as a carefully drawn dogmatic expression. The last remaining statements had such an effect on the judges, that they deemed them worthy of condemnation, without waiting for Pelagius' answer.

Chapter 42 [XVIII.]—The Twelfth Item in the Accusation. Other Heads of Cœlestius' Doctrine Abjured by Pelagius.

For it was objected that in the sixth chapter of Cœlestius' work there was laid down this position: "Men cannot be called sons of God, unless they have become entirely free from all sin." It follows from this statement, that not even the Apostle Paul is a child of God, since he said: "Not as though I had already attained, either were already perfect." In the seventh chapter he makes this statement: "Forgetfulness and ignorance have no connection with sin, as they do not happen through the will, but through necessity;" although David says: "Remember not the sins of my youth, nor my sins of ignorance;" although too, in the law, sacrifices are offered for ignorance, as if for sin. In his tenth chapter he says: "Our will is free, if it needs the help of God; inasmuch as everyone in the possession of his proper will has either something to do or to abstain from doing." In the twelfth he says: "Our victory comes not from God's help, but from our own free will." And this is a conclusion which he was said to draw in the following terms: "The victory is ours, seeing that we took up arms of our own will; just as, on the other hand, being conquered is our own, since it was of our own will that we neglected to arm ourselves." And, after quoting the phrase of the Apostle Peter, "partakers of the divine nature," he is said to have made out of it this argument: "Now if our spirit or soul is unable to be without sin, then even God is subject to sin, since this part of Him, that is to say, the soul, is exposed to sin." In his thirteenth chapter he says: "That pardon is not given to penitents according to the grace and mercy of God, but according to their own merits and effort, since through repentance they have been worthy of mercy."

Chapter 43 [XIX.]—The Answer of the Monk Pelagius and His Profession of Faith.

After all these sentences were read out, the synod said: "What says the monk Pelagius to all these heads of opinion which have been read in his presence? For this holy synod condemns the whole, as does also God's Holy Catholic Church." Pelagius answered: "I say again, that these opinions, even according to their own testimony, are not mine; nor for them, as I have already said, ought I to be held responsible. The opinions which I have confessed to be my own, I maintain are sound; those, however, which I have said are not my own, I reject according to the judgment of this holy synod, pronouncing anathema on every man who opposes and gainsays the doctrines of the Holy Catholic Church. For I believe in the Trinity of the one substance, and I hold all things in accordance with the teaching of the Holy Catholic Church. If indeed any man entertains opinions different from her, let him be anathema."

Chapter 44 [XX.]—The Acquittal of Pelagius.

The synod said: "Now since we have received satisfaction on the points which have come before us touching the monk Pelagius, who has been present; since, too, he gives his consent to the pious doctrines, and even anathematizes everything that is contrary to the Church's faith, we confess him to belong to the communion of the Catholic Church."

Chapter 45 [XXI.]—Pelagius' Acquittal Becomes Suspected.

If these are the proceedings by which Pelagius' friends rejoice that he was exculpated, we, on our part, — since he certainly took much pains to prove that we were well affected towards him, by going so far as to produce even our private letters to him, and reading them at the trial, —undoubtedly wish and desire his salvation in Christ; but about his exculpation, which is rather believed than clearly shown, we ought not to be in a hurry to exult. When I say this, indeed, I do not charge the judges either with negligence or connivance, or with consciously holding unsound doctrine—which they most certainly would be the very last to entertain. But although by their sentence Pelagius is held by those who are on terms of fullest and closest intimacy with him to have been deservedly acquitted, with the approval and commendation of his judges, he certainly does not appear to me to have been cleared of the charges brought against him. They conducted his trial as of one whom they knew nothing of, especially in the absence of those who had prepared the indictment against him, and were quite unable to examine him with diligence and care; but, despite this inability, they completely destroyed the heresy itself, as even the defenders of his perverseness must allow, if they only follow the judgment through its particulars. As for those persons, however, who well know what Pelagius has been in the habit of teaching, or who have had to oppose his contentious efforts, or those who, to their joy, have escaped from his erroneous doctrine, how can they possibly help suspecting him, when they read the affected confession, wherein he acknowledges past errors, but so expresses himself as if he had never entertained any other opinion than those which he stated in his replies to the satisfaction of the judges?

Chapter 46 [XXII.]—How Pelagius Became Known to Augustin; Cœlestius Condemned at Carthage.

Now, that I may especially refer to my own relation to him, I first became acquainted with Pelagius' name, along with great praise of him, at a distance, and when he was living at Rome. Afterwards reports began to reach us, that he disputed against the grace of God. This caused me much pain, for I could not refuse to believe the statements of my informants; but yet I was desirous of ascertaining information on the matter either from himself or from some treatise of his, that, in case I should have to discuss the question with him, it should be on grounds which he could not disown. On his arrival, however, in Africa, he was in my absence kindly received on our coast of Hippo, where, as I found from our brethren, nothing whatever of this kind was heard from him; because he left earlier than was expected. On a subsequent occasion, indeed, I caught a glimpse of him, once or twice, to the best of my recollection, when I was very much occupied in preparing for the conference which we were to hold with the heretical Donatists; but he hastened away across the sea. Meanwhile the doctrines connected with his name were warmly maintained, and passed from mouth to mouth, among his reputed followers—to such an extent that Cœlestius found his way before an ecclesiastical tribunal, and reported opinions well suited to his perverse character. We thought it would be a better way of proceeding against them, if, without mentioning any names of individuals, the errors themselves were met and refuted; and the men might thus be brought to a right mind by the fear of a condemnation from the Church rather than be punished by the actual condemnation. And so both by books and by popular discussions we ceased not to oppose the evil doctrines in question.

Chapter 47 [XXIII.]—Pelagius' Book, Which Was Sent by Timasius and Jacobus to Augustin, Was Answered by the Latter in His Work "On Nature and Grace."

But when there was actually placed in my hands, by those faithful servants of God and honorable men,

Timasius and Jacobus, the treatise in which Pelagius dealt with the question of God's grace, it became very evident to me—too evident, indeed, to admit of any further doubt—how hostile to salvation by Christ was his poisonous perversion of the truth. He treated the subject in the shape of an objection started, as if by an opponent, in his own terms against himself; for he was already suffering a good deal of obloquy from his opinions on the question, which he now appeared to solve for himself in no other way than by simply describing the grace of God as nature created with a free will, occasionally combining therewith either the help of the law, or even the remission of sins; although these additional admissions were not plainly made, but only sparingly suggested by him. And yet, even under these circumstances, I refrained from inserting Pelagius' name in my work, wherein I refuted this book of his; for I still thought that I should render a prompter assistance to the truth if I continued to preserve a friendly relation to him, and so to spare his personal feelings, while at the same time I showed no mercy, as I was bound not to show it, to the productions of his pen. Hence, I must say, I now feel some annoyance, that in this trial he somewhere said: "I anathematize those who hold these opinions, or have at any time held them." He might have been contented with saying, "Those who hold these opinions," which we should have regarded in the light of a self-censure; but when he went on to say, "Or have at any time held them," in the first place, how could he dare to condemn so unjustly those harmless persons who no longer hold the errors, which they had learnt either from others, or actually from himself? And, in the second place, who among all those persons that were aware of the fact of his not only having held the opinions in question, but of his having taught them, could help suspecting, and not unreasonably, that he must have acted insincerely in condemning those who now hold those opinions, seeing that he did not hesitate to condemn in the same strain and at the same moment those also who had at any time previously held them, when they would be sure to remember that they had no less a person than himself as their instructor in these errors? There are, for instance, such persons as Timasius and Jacobus, to say nothing of any others. How can he with unblushing face look at them, his dear friends (who have never relinquished their love of him) and his former disciples? These are the persons to whom I addressed the work in which I replied to the statements of his book. I think I ought not to pass over in silence the style and tone which they observed towards me in their correspondence, and I have here added a letter of theirs as a sample.

Chapter 48 [XXIV.]—A Letter Written by Timasius and Jacobus to Augustin on Receiving His Treatise "On Nature and Grace."

"To his lordship, the truly blessed and deservedly venerable father, Bishop Augustin, Timasius and Jacobus send greeting in the Lord. We have been so greatly refreshed and strengthened by the grace of God, which your word has ministered to us, my lord, our truly blessed and justly venerated father, that we may with the utmost sincerity and propriety say, 'He sent His word and healed them.' We have found, indeed, that your holiness has so thoroughly sifted the contents of his little book as to astonish us with the answers with which even the slightest points of his error have been confronted, whether it be on matters which every Christian ought to rebut, loathe, and avoid, or on those in which he is not with sufficient certainty found to have erred, —although even in these he has, with incredible subtlety, suggested his belief that God's grace should be kept out of sight. There is, however, one consideration which affects us under so great a benefit, —that this most illustrious gift of the grace of God has, however slowly, so fully shone out upon us. If, indeed, it has happened that some are removed from the influence of this clearest light of truth, whose blindness required its illumination, yet even to them, we doubt not, the same grace will find its steady way, however late, by the merciful favor of that God 'who will have all men to be saved and to come unto the knowledge of the truth.' As for ourselves, indeed, thanks to that loving spirit which is in you, we have, in consequence of your instruction, some time since thrown off our subjection to his errors; but we still have even now cause for continued gratitude in the fact that, as we have been informed, the false opinions which we formerly believed are now becoming apparent to others—a way of escape opening out to them in the extremely precious discourse of your holiness." Then, in another hand: "May the mercy of our God keep your blessedness in safety, and mindful of us, for His eternal glory."

Chapter 49 [XXV.]—Pelagius' Behavior Contrasted with that of the Writers of the Letter.

If now that man, too, were to confess that he had once been implicated in this error as a person possessed, but that he now anathematized all that hold these opinions, whoever should withhold his congratulation from him, now that he was in possession of the way of truth, would surely surrender all the bowels of love. As the case, however, now stands, he has not only not acknowledged his liberation from his pestilential error; but, as if that were a small thing, he has gone on to anathematize men who have reached that freedom, who love him so well that they would fain desire his own emancipation. Amongst these are those very men who have expressed their good-will towards him in the letter, which they forwarded to me. For he it was whom they had chiefly in view when they said how much they were affected at the fact of my having at last written that work. "If, indeed, it has happened," they say, "that some are removed from the influence of this clearest light of truth, whose blindness required its illumination, yet even to them," they go on to remark, "we doubt not, the selfsame grace will find its way, by the merciful favor of God." Any name, or names, even they, too, thought it desirable as yet to suppress, in order that, if friendship still lived on, the error of the friends might the more surely die.

Chapter 50. —Pelagius Has No Good Reason to Be Annoyed If His Name Be at Last Used in the Controversy, and He Be Expressly Refuted.

But now if Pelagius thinks of God, if he is not ungrateful for His mercy in having brought him before this tribunal of the bishops, that thus he might be saved from the hardihood of afterwards defending these anathematized opinions, and be at once led to acknowledge them as deserving of abhorrence and rejection, he will be more thankful to us for our book, in which, by mentioning his name, we shall open the wound in order to cure it, than for one in which we were afraid to cause him pain, and, in fact, only produced irritation,—a result which causes us regret. Should he, however, feel angry with us, let him reflect how unfair such anger is; and, in order to subdue it, let him ask God to give him that grace which, in this trial, he has confessed to be necessary for each one of our actions, that so by His assistance he may gain a real victory. For of what use to him are all those great laudations contained in the letters of the bishops, which he thought fit to be mentioned, and even to be read and quoted in his favor, —as if all those persons who heard his strong and, to some extent, earnest exhortations to goodness of life could not have easily discovered how perverse were the opinions which he was entertaining?

Chapter 51 [XXVI.]—The Nature of Augustin's Letter to Pelagius.

For my own part, indeed, in my letter which he produced, I not only abstained from all praises of him, but I even exhorted him, with as much earnestness as I could, short of actually mooting the question, to cultivate right views about the grace of God. In my salutation I called him "lord"—a title which, in our epistolary style, we usually apply even to some persons who are not Christians, —and this without untruth, inasmuch as we do, in a certain sense, owe to all such persons a service, which is yet freedom, to help them in obtaining the salvation which is in Christ. I added the epithet "most beloved;" and as I now call him by this term, so shall I continue to do so, even if he be angry with me; because, if I ceased to retain my love towards him, because of his feeling the anger, I should only injure myself rather than him. I, moreover, styled him "most longed for," because I greatly longed to have a conversation with him in person; for I had already heard that he was endeavoring publicly to oppose grace, whereby we are justified, whenever any mention was made of it. The brief contents of the letter itself indeed show all this; for, after thanking him for the pleasure he gave me by the information of his own health and that of his friends (whose bodily health we are bound of course to wish for, however much we may desire their amendment in other respects), I at once expressed the hope that the Lord would recompense him with such blessings as do not appertain to physical welfare, but which he used to think, and probably still thinks, consist solely in the freedom of the will and his own power,—at the same time, and for this reason, wishing him "eternal life." Then again, remembering the many good and kind wishes he had expressed for me in his letter, which I was answering, I went on to beg of him, too, that he would pray for me, that the Lord would indeed make me such a man as he believed me to be already; that so I might gently remind him, against the opinion he was himself entertaining, that the very righteousness which he had thought worthy to be praised in me was "not of him that wills, nor of him that runs, but of God that shows mercy." This is the substance of that short letter of mine, and such was my purpose when I dictated it. This is a copy of it:

Chapter 52 [XXVII. And XXVIII.]—The Text of the Letter.

"To my most beloved lord, and most longed-for brother Pelagius, Augustin sends greeting in the Lord. I thank you very much for the pleasure you have kindly afforded me by your letter, and for informing me of your good health. May the Lord requite you with blessings, and may you ever enjoy them, and live with Him for evermore in all eternity, my most beloved lord, and most longed-for brother. For my own part, indeed, although I do not admit your high encomiums of me, which the letter of your Benignity conveys, I yet cannot be insensible of the benevolent view you entertain towards my poor deserts; at the same time requesting you to pray for me, that the Lord would make me such a man as you suppose me to be already." Then, in another hand, it follows: "Be mindful of us; may you be safe, and find favor with the Lord, my most beloved lord, and most longed-for brother."

Chapter 53 [XXIX.]—Pelagius' Use of Recommendations.

As to that which I placed in the postscript, —that he might "find favor with the Lord,"—I intimated that this lay rather in His grace than in man's sole will; for I did not make it the subject either of exhortation, or of precept, or of instruction, but simply of my wish. But just in the same way as I should, if I had exhorted or enjoined, or even instructed him, simply have shown that all this appertained to free will, without, however, derogating from the grace of God; so in like manner, when I expressed the matter in the way of a wish, I asserted no doubt the grace of God, but at the same time I did not quench the liberty of the will. Wherefore, then, did he produce this letter at the trial? If he had only from the beginning entertained views in accordance with it, very likely he would not have been at all summoned before the bishops by the brethren, who, with all their kindness of disposition, could yet not help being offended with his perverse contentiousness. Now, however, as I have given on my part an account of this letter of mine, so would they, whose epistles he quoted, explain theirs also, if it were necessary; —they would tell us either what they thought, or what they were ignorant of, or with what purpose they wrote to him. Pelagius, therefore, may boast to his heart's content of the friendship of holy men, he may read their letters recounting his praises, he may produce whatever synodal acts he pleases to attest his own acquittal,—there still stands against him the fact, proved by the testimony of competent witnesses, that he has inserted in his books statements which are opposed to that grace of God whereby we are called and justified; and unless he shall, after true confession, anathematize these statements, and then go on to contradict them both in his writings and discussions, he will certainly seem to all those who have a fuller knowledge of him to have labored in vain in his attempt to set himself right.

Chapter 54 [XXX.]—On the Letter of Pelagius, in Which He Boasts that His Errors Had Been Approved by Fourteen Bishops.

For I will not be silent as to the transactions which took place after this trial, and which rather augment the suspicion against him. A certain epistle found its way into our hands, which was ascribed to Pelagius himself, writing to a friend of his, a presbyter, who had kindly admonished him (as appears from the same epistle) not to allow anyone to separate himself from the body of the Church on his account. Among the other contents of this document, which it would be both tedious and unnecessary to quote here, Pelagius says: "By the sentence of fourteen bishops our statement was received with approbation, in which we affirmed that 'a man is able to be without sin, and easily to keep the commandments of God, if he wishes.' This sentence," says he, "has filled the mouths of the gainsayers with confusion, and has separated asunder the entire set which was conspiring together for evil." Whether, indeed, this epistle was really written by Pelagius, or was composed by somebody in his name, who can fail to see, after what manner this error claims to have achieved a victory, even in the judicial proceedings where it was refuted and condemned? Now, he has adduced the words we have just quoted according to the form in which they occur in his book of "Chapters," as it is called, not in the shape in which they were objected to him at his trial, and even repeated by him in his answer. For even his accusers, through some unaccountable inaccuracy, left out a word in their indictment, concerning which there is no small controversy. They made him say, that "a man is able to be without sin, if he wishes; and, if he wishes, to keep the commandments of God." There is nothing said here about this being "easily" done. Afterwards, when he gave his answer, he spoke thus: "We said, that a man is able to be without sin, and to keep the commandments of God, if he wishes;" he did not then say, "easily keep," but only "keep." So in another place, amongst the statements about which Hilary consulted me, and I gave him my views, it was objected to Pelagius that he had said, "A man is able, if he wishes, to live without sin." To this he himself responded, "That a man is able to be without sin has been said above." Now, on this occasion, we do not find on the part either of those who brought the objection or of him who rebutted it, that the word "easily" was used at all. Then, again, in the narrative of the holy Bishop John, which we have partly quoted above, he says, "When they were importunate and exclaimed, 'He is a heretic, because he says, It is true that a man is able, if he only will, to live without sin;' and then, when we questioned him on this point, he answered, 'I did not say that man's nature has received the power of being impeccable,—but I said, whosoever is willing, in the pursuit of his own salvation, to labor and struggle to abstain from sinning and to walk in the commandments of God, receives the ability to do so from God.' Then, whilst some were whispering, and remarking on the statement of Pelagius, that 'without God's grace man could attain perfection,' I censured the statement, and reminded them, besides, that even the Apostle Paul, after so many labors, —not, indeed, in his own strength, but by the grace of God, —said, 'I labored more abundantly than they all; yet not I, but the grace of God that was with me.'" And so on, as I have already mentioned.

Chapter 55. —Pelagius' Letter Discussed.

What, then, is the meaning of those vaunting words of theirs in this epistle, wherein they boast of having induced the fourteen bishops who sat in that trial to believe not merely that a man has ability but that he has "facility" to abstain from sinning, according to the position laid down in the "Chapters" of this same Pelagius, —when, in the draft of the proceedings, notwithstanding the frequent repetition of the general charge and full consideration bestowed on it, this is nowhere found? How, indeed, can this word fail to contradict the very defense and answer which Pelagius made; since the Bishop John asserted that Pelagius put in this answer in his presence, that "he wished it to be understood that the man who was willing to labor and agonize for his salvation was able to avoid sin," while Pelagius himself, at this time engaged in a formal inquiry and conducting his defense, said, that "it was by his own labor and the grace of God that a man is able to be without sin?" Now, is a thing easy when labor is required to effect it? For I suppose that every man would agree with us in the opinion, that wherever there is labor there cannot be facility. And yet a carnal epistle of windiness and inflation flies forth, and, outrunning in speed the tardy record of the proceedings, gets first into men's hands; so as to assert that fourteen bishops in the East have determined, not only "that a man is able to be without sin, and to keep God's commandments," but "easily to keep." Nor is God's assistance once named: it is merely said, "If he wishes;" so that, of course, as nothing is affirmed of the divine grace, for which the earnest fight was made, it remains that the only thing one reads of in this epistle is the unhappy and self-deceiving—because represented as victorious—human pride. As if the Bishop John, indeed, had not expressly declared that he censured this statement, and that, by the help of three inspired texts of Scripture, he had, as if by thunderbolts, struck to the ground the gigantic mountains of such presumption which they had piled up against the still over towering heights of heavenly grace; or as if again those other bishops who were John's assessors could have borne with Pelagius, either in mind or even in ear, when he pronounced these words: "We said that a man is able to be without sin and to keep the commandments of God, if he wishes," unless he had gone on at once to say: "For the ability to do this God has given to him" (for they were unaware that he was speaking of nature, and not of that grace which they had learnt from the teaching of the apostle); and had afterwards added this qualification: "We never said, however, that any man could be found, who at no time whatever from his infancy to his old age had committed sin, but that if any person were converted from his sins, he could by his own exertion and the grace of God be without sin." Now, by the very fact that in their sentence they used these words, "he has answered correctly, 'that a man can, when he has the assistance and grace of God, be without sin;'" what else did they fear than that, if he denied this, he would be doing a manifest wrong not to man's ability, but to God's grace? It has indeed not been defined when a man may become without sin; it has only been judicially settled, that this result can only be reached by the assisting grace of God; it has not, I say, been defined whether a man, whilst he is in this flesh which lusts against the Spirit, ever has been, or now is, or ever can be, by his present use of reason and free will, either in the full society of man or in monastic solitude, in such a state as to be beyond the necessity of offering up the prayer, not in behalf of others, but for himself personally: "Forgive us our debts;" or whether this gift shall be consummated at the time when "we shall be like Him, when we shall see Him as He is,"—when it shall be said, not by those that are fighting: "I see another law in my members, warring against the law of my mind," but by those that are triumphing: "O death, where is thy victory? O death, where is thy sting?" Now, this is perhaps hardly a question which ought to be discussed between Catholics and heretics, but only among Catholics with a view to a peaceful settlement.

Chapter 56 [XXXI.]—Is Pelagius Sincere?

How, then, can it be believed that Pelagius (if indeed this epistle is his) could have been sincere, when he acknowledged the grace of God, which is not nature with its free will, nor the knowledge of the law, nor simply the forgiveness of sins, but a something which is necessary to each of our actions; or could have sincerely anathematized everybody who entertained the contrary opinion:—seeing that in his epistle he set forth even the ease wherewith a man can avoid sinning (concerning which no question had arisen at this trial) just as if the judges had come to an agreement to receive even this word, and said nothing about the grace of God, by the confession and subsequent addition of which he escaped the penalty of condemnation by the Church?

Chapter 57 [XXXII.]—Fraudulent Practices Pursued by Pelagius in His Report of the Proceedings in Palestine, in the Paper Wherein He Defended Himself to Augustin.

There is yet another point which I must not pass over in silence. In the paper containing his defense which he sent to me by a friend of ours, one Charus, a citizen of Hippo, but a deacon in the Eastern Church, he has made a statement which is different from what is contained in the Proceedings of the Bishops. Now, these Proceedings, about their contents, are of a higher and firmer tone, and more straightforward in defending the catholic verity in opposition to this heretical pestilence. For, when I read this paper of his, before receiving a copy of the Proceedings, I was not aware that he had made use of those words which he had used at the trial, when he was present for himself; they are few, and there is not much discrepancy, and they do not occasion me much anxiety. [XXXIII.] But I could not help feeling annoyance that he can appear to have defended sundry sentences of Cœlestius, which, from the Proceedings, it is clear enough that he anathematized. Now, some of these he disavowed for himself, simply remarking, that "he was not in any way responsible for them." In his paper, however, he refused to anathematize these same opinions, which are to this effect: "That Adam was created mortal, and that he would have died whether he had sinned or not sinned. That Adam's sin injured only himself, and not the human race. That the law, no less than the gospel, leads us to the kingdom. That new-born infants are in the same condition that Adam was before he fell. That, on the one hand, the entire human race does not die owing to Adam's death and transgression; nor, on the other hand, does the whole human race rise again through the resurrection of Christ. That infants, even if they die unbaptized, have eternal life. That rich men, even if they are baptized, unless they renounce and give up all, have, whatever good they may seem to have done, nothing of it reckoned to them; neither shall they possess the kingdom of heaven." Now, in his paper, the answer which he gives to all this is: "All these statements have not been made by me, even on their own testimony, nor do I hold myself responsible for them." In the Proceedings, however, he expressed himself as follows on these points: "They have not been made by me, as even their testimony shows, and for them I do not feel that I am at all responsible. But yet, for the satisfaction of the holy synod, I anathematize those who either now hold, or have ever held, them." Now, why did he not express himself thus in his paper also? It would not, I suppose, have cost much ink, or writing, or delay; nor have occupied much of the paper itself, if he had done this. Who, however, can help believing that there is a purpose in all this, to pass off this paper in all directions as an abridgment of the Episcopal Proceedings. In consequence of which, men might think that his right still to maintain any of these opinions which he pleased had not been taken away, —because they had been simply laid to his charge but had not received his approbation, nor yet had been anathematized and condemned by him.

Chapter 58. —The Same Continued.

He has, moreover, in this same paper, huddled together afterwards many of the points which were objected against him out of the "Chapters," of Cœlestius' book; nor has he kept distinct, at the intervals which separate them in the Proceedings, the two answers in which he anathematized these very heads; but has substituted one general reply for them all. This, I should have supposed, had been done for the sake of brevity, had I not perceived that he had a very special object in the arrangement which disturbs us. For thus has he closed this answer: "I say again, that these opinions, even according to their own testimony, are not mine; nor, as I have already said, am I to be held responsible for them. The opinions which I have confessed to be my own, I maintain are sound and correct; those, however, which I have said are not my own, I reject according to the judgment of the holy Church, pronouncing anathema on every man that opposes and gainsays the doctrines of the holy and catholic Church; and likewise on those who by inventing false opinions have excited odium against us." This last paragraph the Proceedings do not contain; it has, however, no bearing on the matter which causes us anxiety. By all means let them have his anathema who have excited odium against him by their invention of false opinions. But, when first I read, "Those opinions, however, which I have said are not my own, I reject in accordance with the judgment of the holy Church," being ignorant that any judgment had been arrived at on the point by the Church, since there is here nothing said about it, and I had not then read the Proceedings, I really thought that nothing else was meant than that he promised that he would entertain the same view about the "Chapters" as the Church, which had not yet determined the question, might someday decide respecting them; and that he was ready to reject the opinions which the Church had not yet indeed rejected, but might one day have occasion to reject; and that this, too, was the purport of what he further said: "Pronouncing anathema on every man that opposes and gainsays the doctrines of the holy catholic Church." But in fact, as the Proceedings testify, a judgment of the Church had already been pronounced on these subjects by the fourteen bishops; and it was in accordance with this judgment that he professed to reject all these opinions, and to pronounce his anathema against those persons who, because of the said opinions, were contravening the judgment which had already, as the Proceedings show, been actually settled. For already had the judges asked: "What says the monk Pelagius to all these heads of opinion which have been read in his presence? For this holy synod condemns them, as does also God's holy catholic Church." Now, they who know nothing of all this, and only read this paper of his, are led to suppose that someone or other of these opinions may lawfully be maintained, as if they had not been determined to be contrary to catholic doctrine, and as if Pelagius had declared himself to be ready to hold the same sentiments concerning them which the Church had not as yet determined, but might have to determine. He has not, therefore, expressed himself in this paper, to which we have so often referred, straightforwardly enough for us to discover the fact, of which we find a voucher in the Proceedings, that all those dogmas by means of which this heresy has been stealing along and growing strong with contentious audacity, have been condemned by fourteen bishops presiding in an ecclesiastical synod! Now, if he was afraid that this fact would become known, as is the case, he has more reason for self-correction than for resentment at the vigilance with which we are watching the controversy to the best of our ability, however late. If, however, it is untrue that he had any such fears, and we are only indulging in a suspicion which is natural to man, let him forgive us; but, at the same time, let him continue to oppose and resist the opinions which were rejected by him with anathemas in the proceedings before the bishops, when he was on his defense; for if he now shows any leniency to them, he would seem not only to have believed these opinions formerly, but to be cherishing them still.

Chapter 59 [XXXIV.]—Although Pelagius Was Acquitted, His Heresy Was Condemned.

Now, with respect to this treatise of mine, which perhaps is not unreasonably lengthy, considering the importance and extent of its subject, I have wished to inscribe it to your Reverence, in order that, if it be not displeasing to your mind, it may become known to such persons as I have thought may stand in need of it under the recommendation of your authority, which carries so much more weight than our own poor industry. Thus, it may avail to crush the vain and contentious thoughts of those persons who suppose that, because Pelagius was acquitted, those Eastern bishops who pronounced the judgment approved of those dogmas which are beginning to shed very pernicious influences against the Christian faith, and that grace of God whereby we are called and justified. These the Christian verity never ceases to condemn, as indeed it condemned them even by the authoritative sentence of the fourteen bishops; nor would it, on the occasion in question, have hesitated to condemn Pelagius too, unless he had anathematized the heretical opinions with which he was charged. But now, while we render to this man the respect of brotherly affection (and we have all along expressed with all sincerity our anxiety for him and interest in him), let us observe, with as much brevity as is consistent with accuracy of observation, that, notwithstanding the undoubted fact of his having been acquitted by a human verdict, the heresy itself has ever been held worthy of condemnation by divine judgment, and has actually been condemned by the sentence of these fourteen bishops of the Eastern Church.

Chapter 60 [XXXV.]—The Synod's Condemnation of His Doctrines.

This is the concluding clause of their judgment. The synod said: "Now forasmuch as we have received satisfaction in these inquiries from the monk Pelagius, who has been present, who yields assent to godly doctrines, and rejects and anathematizes those which are contrary to the Church, we confess him still to belong to the communion of the catholic Church." Now, there are two facts concerning the monk Pelagius here contained with entire perspicuity in this brief statement of the holy bishops who judged him: one, that "he yields assent to godly doctrines;" the other, that "he rejects and anathematizes those which are contrary to the Church." Because these two concessions, Pelagius was pronounced to be "in the communion of the catholic Church." Let us, in pursuit of our inquiry, briefly recapitulate the entire facts, in order to discover what were the words he used which made those two points so clear, as far as men were able at the moment to form a judgment as to what were manifest points. For among the allegations which were made against him, he is said to have rejected and anathematized, as "contrary," all the statements which in his answer he denied were his. Let us, then, summarize the whole case as far as we can.

Chapter 61. —History of the Pelagian Heresy. The Pelagian Heresy Was Raised by Sundry Persons Who Affected the Monastic State.

Since it was necessary that the Apostle Paul's prediction should be accomplished,—"There must be also heresies among you, that they which are approved may be made manifest among you,"—after the older heresies, there has been just now introduced, not by bishops or presbyters or any rank of the clergy, but by certain would-be monks, a heresy which disputes, under color of defending free will, against the grace of God which we have through our Lord Jesus Christ; and endeavors to overthrow the foundation of the Christian faith of which it is written, "By one man, death, and by one man the resurrection of the dead; for as in Adam all die, even so in Christ shall all be made alive;" and denies God's help in our actions, by affirming that, "in order to avoid sin and to fulfil righteousness, human nature can be sufficient, seeing that it has been created with free will; and that God's grace lies in the fact that we have been so created as to be able to do this by the will, and in the further fact that God has given to us the assistance of His law and commandments, and also in that He forgives their past sins when men turn to Him;" that "in these things alone is God's grace to be regarded as consisting, not in the help He gives to us for each of our actions,"—"seeing that a man can be without sin, and keep God's commandments easily if he wishes."

Chapter 62. —The History Continued. Cœlestius Condemned at Carthage by Episcopal Judgment. Pelagius Acquitted by Bishops in Palestine, in Consequence of His Deceptive Answers; But Yet His Heresy Was Condemned by Them.

After this heresy had deceived a great many persons, and was disturbing the brethren whom it had failed to deceive, one Cœlestius, who entertained these sentiments, was brought up for trial before the Church of Carthage, and was condemned by a sentence of the bishops. Then, a few years afterwards, Pelagius, who was said to have been this man's instructor, having been accused of holding his heresy, found also his way before an episcopal tribunal. The indictment was prepared against him by the Gallican bishops, Heros and Lazarus, who were, however, not present at the proceedings, and were excused from attendance owing to the illness of one of them. After all the charges were duly recited, and Pelagius had met them by his answers, the fourteen bishops of the province of Palestine pronounced him, in accordance with his answers, free from the perversity of this heresy; while yet without hesitation condemning the heresy itself. They approved indeed of his answer to the objections, that "a man is assisted by a knowledge of the law, towards not sinning; even as it is written, 'He hath given them a law for a help;'" but yet they disapproved of this knowledge of the law being that grace of God concerning which the Scripture says: "Who shall deliver me from the body of this death? The grace of God through Jesus Christ our Lord." Nor did Pelagius say absolutely: "All men are ruled by their own will," as if God did not rule them; for he said, when questioned on this point: "This I stated in the interest of the freedom of our will; God is its helper, whenever it makes choice of good. Man, however, when sinning, is himself in fault, as being under the direction of his free will." They approved, moreover, of his statement, that "in the day of judgment no forbearance will be shown to the ungodly and sinners, but they will be punished in everlasting fires;" because in his defense he said, "that he had made such an assertion in accordance with the gospel, in which it is written concerning sinners, 'These shall go away into eternal punishment, but the righteous into life eternal.'" But he did not say, all sinners are reserved for eternal punishment, for then he would evidently have run counter to the apostle, who distinctly states that some of them will be saved, "yet so as by fire." When also Pelagius said that "the kingdom of heaven was promised even in the Old Testament," they approved of the statement, because he supported himself by the testimony of the prophet Daniel, who thus wrote: "The saints shall take the kingdom of the Most High." They understood him, in this statement of his, to mean by the term "Old Testament," not simply the Testament which was made on Mount Sinai, but the entire body of the canonical Scriptures which had been given before the coming of the Lord. His allegation, however, that "a man is able to be without sin, if he wishes," was not approved by the bishops in the sense which he had evidently meant it to bear in his book—as if this was solely in a man's power by free will (for it was contended that he must have meant no less than this by his saying: "if he wishes"),—but only in the sense which he actually gave to the passage on the present occasion in his answer; in the very sense, indeed, in which the episcopal judges mentioned the subject in their own interlocution with especial brevity and clearness, that a man is able to be without sin with the help and grace of God. But still it was left undetermined when the saints were to attain to this state of perfection, —whether in the body of this death, or when death shall be swallowed up in victory.

Chapter 63. —The Same Continued. The Dogmas of Cœlestius Laid to the Charge of Pelagius, as His Master, and Condemned.

Of the opinions which Cœlestius has said or written, and which were objected against Pelagius, because they were the dogmas of his disciple, he acknowledged some as entertained also by himself; but, in his vindication, he said that he held them in a different sense from that which was alleged in the indictment. One of these opinions was thus stated: "Before the advent of Christ some men lived holy and righteous lives." Cœlestius, however, was stated to have said that "they lived sinless lives." Again, it was objected that Cœlestius declared "the Church to be without spot and wrinkle." Pelagius, however, said in his reply, "that he had made such an assertion, but as meaning that the Church is by the laver cleansed from every spot and wrinkle, and that in this purity the Lord would have her continue." Respecting that statement of Cœlestius: "That we do more than is commanded us in the law and the gospel," Pelagius urged in his own vindication, that "he spoke concerning virginity," of which Paul says: "I have no commandment of the Lord." Another objection alleged that Cœlestius had maintained that "every individual has the ability to possess all powers and graces," thus annulling that "diversity of gifts" which, the apostle sets forth. Pelagius, however, answered, that "he did not annul the diversity of gifts, but declared that God gives to the man who has proved himself worthy to receive them, all graces, even as He gave the Apostle Paul."

Chapter 64. —How the Bishops Cleared Pelagius of Those Charges.

These four dogmas, thus connected with the name of Cœlestius, were therefore not approved by the bishops in their judgment, in the sense in which Cœlestius was said to have set them forth but in the sense which Pelagius gave to them in his reply. For they saw clearly enough, that it is one thing to be without sin, and another thing to live holily and righteously, as Scripture testifies that some lived even before the coming of Christ. And that although the Church here on earth is not without spot or wrinkle, she is yet both cleansed from every spot and wrinkle by the laver of regeneration, and in this state the Lord would have her continue. And continue she certainly will, for without doubt she shall reign without spot or wrinkle in an everlasting felicity. And that the perpetual virginity, which is not commanded, is unquestionably more than the purity of wedded life, which is commanded—although virginity is persevered in by many persons, who, notwithstanding, are not without sin. And that all those graces which he enumerates in a certain passage were possessed by the Apostle Paul; and yet, for all that, either they could quite understand, in regard to his having been worthy to receive them, that the merit was not according to his works, but rather, in some way, according to predestination (for the apostle says himself: "I am not meet to be called an apostle;") or else their attention was not arrested by the sense which Pelagius gave to the word, as he himself viewed it. Such are the points on which the bishops pronounced the agreement of Pelagius with the doctrines of godly truth.

Chapter 65. —Recapitulation of What Pelagius Condemned.

Let us now, by a like recapitulation, bestow a little more attention on those subjects which the bishops said he rejected and condemned as "contrary;" for herein especially lies the whole of that heresy. We will entirely pass over the strange terms of adulation which he is reported to have put into writing in praise of a certain widow; these he denied having ever inserted in any of his writings, or ever given utterance to, and he anathematized all who held the opinions in question not indeed as heretics, but as fools. The following are the wild thickets of this heresy, which we are sorry to see shooting out buds, nay growing into trees, day by day:—"That Adam was made mortal, and would have died whether he had sinned or not; that Adam's sin injured only himself, and not the human race; that the law no less than the gospel leads to the kingdom; that new-born infants are in the same condition that Adam was before the transgression; that the whole human race does not, on the one hand, die in consequence of Adam's death and transgression, nor, on the other hand, does the whole human race rise again through the resurrection of Christ; that infants, even if they die unbaptized, have eternal life; that rich men, even if baptized, unless they renounce and surrender everything, have, whatever good they may seem to have done, nothing of it reckoned to them, neither can they possess the kingdom of God; that God's grace and assistance are not given for single actions, but reside in free will, and in the law and teaching; that the grace of God is bestowed according to our merits, so that grace really lies in the will of man, as he makes himself worthy or unworthy of it; that men cannot be called children of God, unless they have become entirely free from sin; that forgetfulness and ignorance do not come under sin, as they do not happen through the will, but of necessity; that there is no free will, if it needs the help of God, inasmuch as everyone has his proper will either to do something, or to abstain from doing it; that our victory comes not from

God's help, but from free will; that from what Peter says, that 'we are partakers of the divine nature,' it must follow that the soul has the power of being without sin, just in the way that God Himself has." For this have I read in the eleventh chapter of the book, which bears no title of its author, but is commonly reported to be the work of Cœlestius, —expressed in these words: "Now how can anybody," asks the author, "become a partaker of the thing from the condition and power of which he is distinctly declared to be a stranger?" Accordingly, the brethren who prepared these objections understood him to have said that man's soul and God are of the same nature, and to have asserted that the soul is part of God; for thus they understood that he meant that the soul partakes of the same condition and power as God. Moreover, in the last of the objections laid to his charge there occurs this position: "That pardon is not given to penitents according to the grace and mercy of God, but according to their own merits and effort, since through repentance they have been worthy of mercy." Now all these dogmas, and the arguments which were advanced in support of them, were repudiated and anathematized by Pelagius, and his conduct herein was approved of by the judges, who accordingly pronounced that he had, by his rejection and anathema, condemned the opinions in question as contrary to the faith. Let us therefore rejoice—whatever may be the circumstances of the case, whether Cœlestius laid down these theses or not, or whether Pelagius believed them or not—that the injurious principles of this new heresy were condemned before that ecclesiastical tribunal; and let us thank God for such a result, and proclaim His praises.

Chapter 66. —The Harsh Measures of the Pelagians Against the Holy Monks and Nuns Who Belonged to Jerome's Charge.

Certain followers of Pelagius are said to have carried their support of his cause after these judicial proceedings to an incredible extent of perverseness and audacity. They are said to have most cruelly beaten and maltreated the servants and handmaidens of the Lord who lived under the care of the holy presbyter Jerome, slain his deacon, and burnt his monastic houses; whilst he himself, by God's mercy, narrowly escaped the violent attacks of these impious assailants in the shelter of a well-defended fortress. However, I think it better becomes me to say nothing of these matters, but to wait and see what measures our brethren the bishops may deem it their duty to adopt concerning such scandalous enormities; for nobody can suppose that it is possible for them to pass them over without notice. Impious doctrines put forth by persons of this character it is no doubt the duty of all Catholics, however remote their residence, to oppose and refute, and so to hinder all injury from such opinions wheresoever they may happen to find their way; but impious actions it belongs to the discipline of the episcopal authority on the spot to control, and they must be left for punishment to the bishops of the very place or immediate neighborhood, to be dealt with as pastoral diligence and godly severity may suggest. We, therefore, who live at so great a distance, are bound to hope that such a stop may there be put to proceedings of this kind, that there may be no necessity elsewhere of further invoking judicial remedies. But what rather befits our personal activity is so to set forth the truth, that the minds of all those who have been severely wounded by the report, so widely spread everywhere, may be healed by the mercy of God following our efforts. With this desire, I must now at last terminate this work, which, should it succeed, as I hope, in commending itself to your mind, will, I trust, with the Lord's blessing, become serviceable to its readers—recommended to them rather by your name than by my own, and through your care and diligence receiving a wider circulation.

www.ingramcontent.com/pod-product-compliance
Lightning Source LLC
Chambersburg PA
CBHW052106070526
44584CB00017B/2360